# A Slice Of History

CW00860329

★ ★ ★ ★ ★ ★ ★ ★ ★ ★

## THE BEST CAKE RECIPES FROM AMERICA'S SWEET PAST

### By: Julie Schoen

*For my mom, whose cakes continue to delight and amaze,
showing each person she loves just how special they really are to her.
I love you Mom!*

**Disclaimer Notice:**

Please note the information contained within this document is for educational purposes only.

Every attempt has been made to provide accurate, up to date and reliable complete information no warranties of any kind are expressed or implied. Readers acknowledge that the author is not engaging in rendering legal, financial or professional advice.

By reading any document, the reader agrees that under no circumstances are we responsible for any losses, direct or indirect, which are incurred as a result of use of the information contained within this document, including – but not limited to errors, omissions, or inaccuracies.

# Contents

# A Piece Of Cake: Author's Introduction

A few months ago I baked a very special cake for my son's first birthday. I envisioned grand cakes, themed to my and my husband's favorite childhood book, *Where The Wild Things Are*, perfect in appearance, delightful in taste, just like the ones my mom baked for me and my brothers and sisters when we were little. As his birthday crept closer I began to panic, changing my mind again and again about how I would go about attempting this birthday cake feat. Would I buy figurines or make them? Would the entire cake be edible or should I use other material to build the forest? How many Wild Things should there be? Where would I put the candle? Like many things in my life, I was over thinking but couldn't stop myself.

I blinked and it was the day before his birthday party; I was nowhere closer to figuring out just how to construct this special cake than I was months ago. Sadly, I let go of my lofty goal and settled on something simple – cupcakes for the family and a small, layered cake for my son to enjoy (aka destroy).

The lemon batter was quickly poured into my two four-inch baking pans the morning of his party, me racing out of the kitchen to see my little man dancing in his crib and shouting "Puppy!" at the sight of our Basset Hound coming into his room, oblivious that this day was a very special type of day. The cakes cooled on a wire rack while I made the cupcakes, same lemon batter only they were to be filled with blueberry jam as a special (and unfortunately very messy) surprise for family. The first layer of my son's cake was placed on a cake platter and topped with the messy jam (Note: the messier the cake the better the pictures it turns out). With the second layer placed on top I began to frost the cake with bright blue frosting. I was absorbed in making each stroke of my knife perfect, getting upset when the neon frosting decided to have a mind of its own. Frustration was creeping in and having an unsettling effect on my now shaking hands.

And then I felt something on my leg – a little tug from a little boy. "Up!" For a split-second I thought about not picking him up, about wanting to finish the cake perfectly with no distractions. About to call my husband to come get him I changed my mind. Seeing the delight in his face as he was boosted into my arms to catch a glimpse of what I was doing changed everything. The idea of the perfect cake no longer mattered. With my son in one arm I finished frosting the cake rapidly. I gave my son a handful of sprinkles and he threw them on the cake (and counter and floor) with gusto.

We laughed together for a brief moment before he ran off to discover a new game. I placed the cake in the refrigerator looking at it with new eyes. No, it was not perfect and it definitely wasn't what I had in mind when I thought about this day months ago. But when I looked at it sitting on the top shelf of my refrigerator, thinking about what it meant, and about singing Happy Birthday to my son with the "1" candle on top later that afternoon, I realized that this is why we make cakes. We make cakes for memories, to show people we love them or that we are thinking of them. We make cakes because it expresses what is sometimes hard to put into words. We make cakes because we are human.

I look back on all of the cakes my mom baked when I was little, birthday cakes, holiday cakes, cakes to celebrate, and cakes to cheer us up, and I now understand that behind each cake, whether it was perfect or not, was something much more important than just dessert. In between the layers of each cake, sifted into the flour, and whisked until creamy was love.

# A Slice Of History And On Becoming Baking Betty

Betty has been the All-American girl name since the 1800's. The name saw its heyday in the early 1900's, being given to thousands of little girls including Betty White, Betty Grable, and Betty Ford to literally name a few. The association between "baking" and "Betty" most likely became popular during the 1950's when the company Betty Crocker was taking over the baking industry with cookbooks, cake mixes, flour, and more. According to the company's history, the name "Betty" was chosen in 1921 because it epitomized the image of the American homemaker, cheery, wise, and godly.

Today baking has become much more than a homemaker's duty. Baking can turn a house into a home, bring back fond memories, act as a form of stress-relief, express someone's feelings, and even be a creative outlet for culinary geniuses (or those of us who just like to have fun with a decorator's bag!)

But there comes a point in everyone's life that in order to really understand something you have to quit dilly-dallying, muster up the confidence, and just do it! I am under the impression that convincing you to go bake a cake isn't something that will take convincing so rather than delaying the inevitable I think it is time to set you loose in the kitchen. The best Baking Betties, as we all know, are the ones who love to bake, bake often, and bake for reasons other than making the perfect cake (although, as you know, a perfect cake is definitely not a bad thing!) So pick out your favorite recipes below (or better yet, try them all in historical order – from 1606 to 1997!), gather up some loved ones to lick the beaters, and get baking Betty!

# An American Timeline of Cakes

★ ★ ★ ★ ★ ★ ★ ★ ★ ★

EUROPE MAKES ITS FIRST PERMANENT
SETTLEMENT IN NORTH AMERICA
1565

★ ★ ★ ★ ★ ★ ★ ★ ★ ★

# Maple Syrup

1606

During the early exploration of the United States in the seventeenth century, French explorers noted in their journals the unique process used by the Native Americans to extract, collect, and distill maple sap from trees. And while the Native Americans did create a variety of sugar from this sap, they did not enjoy maple syrup, as we know it today, because they were required to boil it past this point in order to store it more easily. It wasn't until 1880 that American sugar producers became syrup producers thanks to the readily available and affordability of equipment like evaporator pans, buckets, and spouts. At this time the import tax on cane sugar had been removed. And while this killed the maple sugar industry it set the stage for the growth and success of the still wildly popular American maple syrup market.

## DOUBLE MAPLE FROSTED CAKE
*Serves 10*

### Ingredients

- ★ 3 cups flour
- ★ 1 tablespoon baking better
- ★ 1 ¼ teaspoon salt
- ★ ½ cup unsalted butter, at room temperature
- ★ 2½ tablespoons vegetable shortening, at room temperature
- ★ 2 cups Grade B pure American maple syrup
- ★ 3 large egg yolks

★  1 large egg
★  1½ cups milk

For the frosting
★  3 cups confectioner's sugar
★  8 ounces cream cheese, at room temperature
★  ½ cup unsalted butter, at room temperature
★  2½ tablespoons maple syrup

Directions
-  Preheat your oven's temperature to 325 degrees F.  Grease 2 8" round cake pans and then
   line the bottoms with parchment paper.  Using butter, grease the top of the parchment
   paper to make sure that your cake does not stick.  Dust the pans with flour and then set
   aside.

-  In a medium size bowl sift together the flour, baking powder, and salt.  In a large bowl,
   combine the butter and shortening, beating with an electric mixer until it becomes fluffy.
   Pour the maple syrup into the butter mixture and continue beating with the mixer until
   it becomes smooth (2 to 3 minutes).  As you add the eggs to this mixture, be sure to add
   just one egg at a time, mixing with the blender as you go.

-  Add the flour mixture 1 cup at a time to the creamed mixture, alternating with an addition
   of a ½ cup of milk.  Evenly distribute the batter between the prepared pans, using a wet
   spatula to even the tops.  Place the cakes in the preheated oven and bake for 50 minutes
   or until a toothpick inserted into the center of the cake comes out clean.  When finished
   baking, allow the cakes to cool in the pans (not on the stove) for 15 to 20 minutes.  Before
   removing the cakes from the pan, run a butter knife around the edges to loosen.  Then flip
   the cakes onto cooling racks, taking off the parchment paper from the bottom.

-  As the cakes continue to cool prepare the frosting.  In a medium bowl sift the confectioner's
   sugar.  In a large bowl, beat together the cream cheese and butter with an electric mixer.
   Then add the sifted confectioner's sugar, beating with the mixer for no more than 60
   seconds or until it is smooth.

-  Once the cakes are completely cool, carefully remove the domed top of each cake with a
   serrated knife so that they don't slide or wobble as you frost.  Set the first cake on a serving
   platter and frost the top and sides with a slightly wet knife.  Then add the second cake,
   frosting just as you did the first.

-  The cake should be served at room temperature and is best eaten within a day.

# Smith Island

## 1632

England granted the first charter to settle what we now know as Maryland in 1632. George Calvert, the recipient of the charter, became the first Lord Baltimore. The name Maryland was chosen to honor Henrietta Maria, the wife of King Charles I. Smith Island, the only inhabited island in Maryland's Chesapeake Bay, was not settled until a few decades later, although it was discovered by Captain John Smith (although this is not whom the island is named for) in 1608 via his ship the Phoenix.

Smith Island began to be settled in the late 1650s by groups of English and Dutch settlers who, of course, brought with them their unique culture and, equally important, their unique baking traditions. The island received its name from the landowner Henry Smith, one of the first to successfully settle.

The Smith Island Cake is Maryland's official state cake and, according to residents of the island, it came with the settlers, making it a nearly four-century tradition that, while adapted to each generation's kitchen advancements, has clearly withstood the test of time. What started as a fudgy four-layer cake transformed into a sky-high cake of 12 or more layers thanks to the competitive nature of Smith Island's very own Baking Betties.

## TRADITIONAL SMITH ISLAND CAKE
*Serves 16*

### Ingredients

- ★ 1 cup unsalted butter, at room temperature
- ★ 3 cups flour
- ★ ½ teaspoon salt
- ★ 1½ teaspoons baking powder
- ★ 2¼ cups sugar
- ★ 5 large eggs
- ★ 1 cup evaporated milk
- ★ 2 teaspoons pure vanilla extract
- ★ ½ - ¾ cup water

### For the frosting

- ★ 2 cups sugar
- ★ 1 cup evaporated milk
- ★ 6 ounces unsweetened chocolate, chopped
- ★ ½ cup unsalted butter
- ★ 1 teaspoon pure vanilla extract

### Directions

- Preheat your oven's temperature to 350 degrees F. Grease as many 9" round cake pans as you have available (2 to 10). If working with fewer pans, be sure to re-grease them each time before adding more batter.

- In a large bowl, use a sifter to combine the flour, salt, and baking powder. In another large bowl, beat together the butter and sugar with an electric mixer on medium speed. Once the butter mixture has become creamy, beat in the eggs one at a time. Turn your electric mixer to low and add the sifted flour mixture 1 cup at a time. Once all of the flour mixture has been incorporated begin to add the evaporated milk, vanilla, and water.

- Add 2/3 cup of batter to each prepared cake pan, spreading it evenly with a slightly wet spatula. Bake each layer for 8 minutes in the preheated oven. As the layers begin to finish baking, use a small knife to loosen the edges from the pan and carefully invert onto cooling racks. If reusing pans for other layers, be sure to clean and re-grease first.

- Meanwhile, prepare the frosting by placing the sugar and evaporated milk in a medium size saucepan. Turn the oven's surface heat to medium-low and stir in the chocolate and butter. Stir the mixture constantly until both the chocolate and butter have melted. Then bump the heat up to medium and cook for 12 to 14 minutes, stirring occasionally. Take the frosting off the heat and stir in the vanilla. As the frosting cools it will thicken.

- To construct the cake place the bottom layer on a serving plate. Frost the top of the cake, not worrying too much if pieces of the cake tear since the frosting will cover it (no one but you will ever know – I promise!)  Continue stacking the cake layers one on top of another, frosting with a generous amount of chocolate goodness in between, until you have finished.

# Old Hartford Election

1771

According to the detailed records from Connecticut's 1771 gubernatorial election, Mrs. Ledlie was responsible for making the "great" cake for the enjoyment of all who travelled to Hartford. Election Day in the eighteenth century was a certified holiday, one of the new popular secular holidays since religious holidays at the time were banished by the Puritans. Connecticut is logically considered the birthplace of election cake because it was one of the first colonies given the right to vote for its own governor. The cake baked for the holiday was meant to accompany town "drinkings", a public type of festival enjoyed by all since work was set-aside for the day.

The great cake baked by Mrs. Ledlie in 1771 was indeed great with estimates of it being more than a yard wide and over a foot tall. It wasn't until 1796, however, after the tradition of baking an Election Day cake had become more popular, that an official recipe was published in Amelia Simmons's famous cookbook, American Cookery. This recipe calls for over thirty quarts of flour, a bushel. By the 1800's, as more and more Americans began baking cakes similar to Mrs. Ledlie's original, the Election Day cake became smaller in size although still grand in taste.

## OLD BUT NEW HARTFORD ELECTION CAKE
*Serves 10*

### Ingredients
- ★ 4 cups flour
- ★ 1 cup unsalted butter

- ★  1 ½ cups cane sugar
- ★  ¾ cup homemade yeast (use a starter from a bread, like sourdough)
- ★  1 egg, whisked
- ★  1 cup milk, warmed slightly
- ★  1 ½ cups raisins
- ★  2 teaspoons freshly grated nutmeg
- ★  ¼ cup red wine
- ★  ¼ cup brandy

For the icing

- ★  1 cup cane sugar
- ★  3 teaspoons brandy
- ★  2 teaspoons red wine
- ★  ¼ teaspoon confectioner's sugar

Directions

- Begin the night before by cutting the butter into the flour in a large bowl – a pastry blender works well for this. Stir in the warm milk, the homemade yeast, and ¾ cup of sugar. Then add in the beaten egg. Use a large wooden spoon to create a sticky dough, using your hands (like kneading) if necessary. Place a damp towel over the dough and allow it to rise over night (about 12 hours).

- Prepare a 13x9" pan by greasing it; set aside. Preheat your oven's temperature to 300 degrees F.

- Once the dough has risen to the point that it looks a little fluffy, work in the remaining ¾ cup of sugar, the grated nutmeg, the raisins, the wine, and the brandy. Place the dough in the prepare pan and cover with a towel. Set the pan on top of the warm oven and allow the dough to rise for 3 to 4 hours or until it becomes fluffy again. As the dough finishes rising, increase your oven's temperature to 350. Bake the cake in the oven for 45 to 50 minutes or until a toothpick inserted in the center comes out clean.

- As the bake cakes prepare the icing by placing all of the ingredients in a bowl and beating with an electric mixer. You can adjust the consistency of the icing by adding more confectioners' sugar as necessary.

- Allow the cake to cool for several minutes before removing it from the pan and transferring it to a cooling rack. Allow it to cool another 10 to 15 minutes before icing and serving.

REVOLUTIONARY WAR ENDS WITH THE
SIGNING OF THE PEACE TREATY
1783

BENJAMIN FRANKLIN INVENTS BIFOCAL
EYEGLASSES
1784

AMERICA'S CONSTITUTION IS RATIFIED
1788

# Pound

1796

The British are credited with inventing the Pound Cake in the early 1700's out of pure convenience. In order to make remembering a cake recipe, well, a piece of cake, the Brits came up with the idea of putting a pound of each ingredient (butter, sugar, eggs, and flour), hence the name Pound Cake. And while these cakes are delicious, they are massive, capable of feeding several families in a community at once. In 1796 Amelia Simmons published the first American cookbook, American Cookery. In her cookbook she includes two recipes for Pound Cake, both sticking to the traditional one-pound of each ingredient method.

As the cake gained popularity in the United States it began to adapt to the needs of American women. Not finding it necessary to feed dozens of people with one cake but enjoying the traditional taste of the Pound Cake, recipes began to decrease the amount of ingredients to make a lighter, smaller cake.

## SIMPLE POUND CAKE
*Serves 12*

### Ingredients

- ★ 4 cups flour
- ★ 3 cups sugar
- ★ 2 cups softened butter
- ★ ¾ cup whole milk

★  6 large brown eggs
★  2½ teaspoons vanilla extract

Directions

- Set your oven's temperature to 325 degrees F.  Prepare a 10" tube pan by greasing the bottom and sides and then dusting with flour.

- In a large bowl combine all of the ingredients.  Use an electric mixer on low speed to beat the mixture for 1 minute.  Use a spatula to scrape the sides and then beat the mixture for another 2 minutes, this time on medium speed.  Pour the mixture into the prepared pan and bake in the preheated oven for 90 minutes or until a toothpick inserted into the center of the cake comes out clean.

- When finished baking, place the cake (still in the pan) on a cooling rack for ten minutes.  Carefully invert the pan on the cooling rack, removing the cake.  Before slicing or serving allow the cake to cool for at least an hour.

# Angel Food

1800

The texture of the Angel Food cake is reminiscent of other popular late eighteenth century cakes, like the Silver Cake. In the early nineteenth century, the Pennsylvania Dutch began producing cake molds in mass. As the popularity of cake molds began to increase so did the creation of new cakes that could be made with them. The Angel Food cake, also known as Wedding Cake among the Pennsylvania Dutch, is made with lots of egg whites and no shortening, ingredients which were commonly on hand in American homes around this time.

But because the rotary egg beaters, which made whipping eggs much easier, weren't easily available until the late nineteenth century, some historians believe that this cake was actually created in the South by African American slaves who would have the strength necessary to successfully whip enough air into the egg whites to produce the light and fluffy texture that this cake is known for. Today this cake remains popular in the South and is often prepared after funerals for family and friends.

## SOUTHERN STYLE ANGEL FOOD CAKE
*Serves 10*

### Ingredients
- ★ 2 cups sugar, ground until very fine
- ★ ¼ teaspoon salt
- ★ 1 cup sifted cake flour

★ 12 fresh egg whites, at room temperature
★ 1/3 cup lukewarm water
★ 1 teaspoon almond extract
★ 1 ½ teaspoons cream of tartar

## Directions

- Set your oven's temperature to 350 degrees F.

- In a medium bowl, sift together 1 cup of sugar, the salt, and the flour. In another larger bowl, whisk together the egg whites, water, almond extract, and cream of tartar. After whisking for several minutes begin to beat with a hand mixer on medium speed. Working in small batches, add the remaining cup of sugar while beating constantly. Continue beating until peaks begin to form.

- Use a spatula to fold in the sifted mixture.

- Pour the batter into an ungreased tube pan and bake in the preheated oven for 30 to 35 minutes or until a toothpick inserted into the center of the cake comes out clean. When finished baking, allow the cake to cool in its pan upside down on a cooling rack for 1 to 2 hours. After it has cooled, remove the pan and slice to serve.

- Angel food cake is great on its own but can also be served with fresh seasonal fruit and whipped cream for an extra treat.

★ ★ ★ ★ ★ ★ ★ ★ ★ ★

LEWIS AND CLARKE BEGIN
THEIR EXPEDITION
1804

★ ★ ★ ★ ★ ★ ★ ★ ★ ★

# Jelly Roll

★ ★ ★ ★ ★ ★ ★ ★ ★ ★

1809

The Jelly Roll cake got its start in England much like many traditional American cakes. In the late 1700s recipes for "cream cakes" or "jelly cakes" were gaining popularity in London. These early recipes called for two flat cake, puff pastry, or meringue layers held together with a generous serving of fruit jam. The first documentation of a jelly cake in the United States was the reference to the "jelly cake mould" in an 1809 publication of the New York Gazette.

The Jelly Roll as we know it today, a long sponge cake rolled up with flavorful fruit jam, first appeared in 1852 in a New York journal called the Northern Farmer. The Jelly Roll cake has been known to masquerade under a variety of names, such as the Swiss Roll, Venice Roll, Paris Roll, and Rolled Jelly Cake, although Jelly Roll remains the most common in America.

The recipe below uses rhubarb, one of my grandmother's backyard garden specialties. Although rhubarb pie is what I remember most from my childhood, I am sure she would approve of this sweetened use of her tangy rhubarb. If rhubarb isn't in season, strawberries, cherries, blueberries, and peaches all make wonderful stand-ins in this recipe.

## BACKYARD RHUBARB JELLY ROLL
*Serves 12*

Ingredients
- ★ 6 cups freshly chopped rhubarb
- ★ 3 cups sugar

- ★ 1¾ teaspoons ground cinnamon
- ★ ¼ teaspoon allspice
- ★ 1/8 teaspoon ground cloves
- ★ 4 fresh eggs
- ★ 1 teaspoon almond extract
- ★ ¾ cup flour
- ★ 1 teaspoon baking powder
- ★ ¼ teaspoon salt
- ★ Confectioner's sugar, for serving

## Directions

- Set your oven's temperature to 375 degrees F. Prepare a 15x10" baking pan by lining it with greased waxed paper and set aside.

- Place the chopped rhubarb, 2 cups of the sugar, and spices in a large saucepan over high heat. Once the mixture begins to boil, lower the heat to medium-high, cooking the mixture for 10 to 12 minutes, stirring every few minutes, until the mixture becomes thick with the consistency of jam. Remove the saucepan from the heat and allow the filling to cool completely.

- Beat the eggs in a large bowl with an electric mixer for 2 to 3 minutes. Add the remaining cup of sugar and continue beating for another 2 minutes. Once the mixture thickens, add the almond extract and stir. Add the remaining dry ingredients, folding into the egg mixture. Once all of the batter ingredients have been well incorporated, pour into the prepared baking pan. Bake the cake in the preheated oven for 15 minutes or until the cake is light and springy when touched.

- Dust a clean kitchen towel with confectioner's sugar. Allow the cake to cool for 5 to 10 minutes before removing it from the pan and inverting it onto the towel. Remove the waxed paper from the bottom of the cake and roll in the towel, beginning with the short end. The cake should cool completely rolled in the towel before adding the rhubarb filling.

- Carefully unroll the cake and spread the filling evenly on top. Using the heel of your hands, roll the cake as before. Place the cake on a serving platter, seam down. Use plastic wrap to lightly cover the cake and place in the refrigerator for 1 to 2 hours. Before serving, dust the top of the cake with additional confectioner's sugar.

# Sponge

1829

One of the earliest non-yeasted cakes recorded in history, the Sponge Cake dates back to England in the early 1600s when the author Gervase Markham first published the recipe in his 1915 book The English Huswife. It took over two centuries for a similar recipe to wash up on shore of the United States. The abolitionist and activist Lydia Maria Child published her recipe for Sponge Cake in her 1829 kitchen book called The American Frugal Housewife.

Sponge Cake continues to be one of the most popular cakes in the world, popping up in France, Portugal, and Italy known as the Genoise, pao-de-lo, and the pan di Spagna respectively. Both the chiffon cake and tres leches cake play off the idea of the classic sponge cake.

## VANILLA SPONGE CAKE
*Serves 10*

### Ingredients
- ★ ½ cup flour, plus additional for dusting
- ★ ½ cup cornstarch
- ★ 4 large brown eggs, separated
- ★ 2 teaspoons vanilla extract
- ★ ¾ cup granulated sugar
- ★ 1/8 teaspoon Himalayan sea salt

Directions

- Preheat your oven's temperature to 350 degrees F. Grease a 9" round cake pan and then line with greased parchment paper. Dust the pan with flour and set aside.

- Sift the flour and cornstarch together in a small size bowl.

- Using an electric mixer, preferably one with a whisk attachment, beat the egg yolks, vanilla extract, and half of the sugar on high speed for 4 to 5 minutes or until the mixture begins to thicken and turn pale in color. Pour the mixture into a large bowl.

- In a separate bowl using a clean mixer, beat together the egg whites and salt on medium speed until soft peaks form. Continue mixing and add the other half of the sugar. Beat the sugar into the egg whites for about a minute or until the peaks become stiff. Add this mixture into the egg yolk mixture by gently folding in with a spatula. Working in small batches, begin to add in the flour mixture, folding as before.

- Pour the batter into the prepared cake pan and smooth the top. Place the filled cake pan in the preheated oven and bake for about 40 minutes or until a toothpick inserted into the center of the cake comes out clean. When the cake is finished baking, place the pan on a cooling rack. Once the cake is cool, invert it on a serving dish and slice to serve. If you would like to store the cake for later, cover it in plastic wrap and place in the refrigerator.

- This cake makes a wonderful, modest dessert by itself topped with a dusting of confectioner's sugar, but it can also be used as the base for homemade Tiramisu.

# Wedding

1833

Although the history of wedding cake is difficult to recreate with a simple timeline, there is no question that the American wedding cake has transformed from a simple, modest cake to one of the most elaborate and expensive aspects of a modern wedding. The first well-documented description and recipe for a wedding cake is in Mrs. Child's famous cookbook, The American Frugal Housewife: Dedicated to Those who are Not Ashamed of Economy published in 1833. Her recipe calls for over four pounds of currants, two pounds of raisins and a half a pint of brandy. The frosting is simple, an easy mixture of egg whites and sugar, dried onto the cake in front of a warm fire.

With royalty and the incredibly wealthy aside, the modern wedding cake is far more extravagant than anything baked up in the 19th century or before. Most couples will spend between $500 and $1,000 on their special cake, although it is not unheard of for couples to spend far more in order to create their desired dessert. In 2002, Liza Minnelli and David Gest are rumored to have spent over $40,000 on their wedding cake, a massive feast for the eyes covered in freshly cut roses, black ribbon, and well-over five-feet tall. Chelsea Clinton and Marc Mezvinsky spent $11,000 on their cake alone, but Kate Middleton and Prince William literally take the cake on overall expense with their $80,000 post-ceremony dessert.

More important than simply being extravagant, today's wedding cake tradition allows the bride and groom to express themselves, the style and type of cake acting as a mirror into the couple's personalities, hobbies, heritage, and wedding theme. It is not uncommon to discover that the wedding cake is not even a cake at all considering the rising popularity of dessert bars, wedding pies, and even wedding ice cream sundaes.

## TIERED GARDEN ORANGE ALMOND WEDDING CAKE WITH CRYSTALLIZED PANSIES
*Serves 85*

### Ingredients

- ★ 4 cups unsalted butter, softened
- ★ 6 cups granulated sugar
- ★ 12 large brown eggs, fresh
- ★ 8 cups cake flour
- ★ 1 ½ cups whole milk
- ★ 4¼ teaspoons pure vanilla extract
- ★ 1 ½ teaspoons orange extract
- ★ ¾ cup orange liqueur

### For the frosting

- ★ 1½ cups unsalted butter, softened
- ★ 24 ounces cream cheese, softened
- ★ 48 ounces confectioner's sugar, sifted
- ★ 6 tablespoons almond liqueur

### For the filling

- ★ 36 ounces orange preserves

### For the crystallized pansies

- ★ 16 ounces confectioner's sugar, sifted
- ★ 3 tablespoons meringue powder
- ★ 1¼ cups water
- ★ 10 dozen pansies, in desired colors
- ★ 3 dozen pansy leaves
- ★ 16 ounces superfine sugar

### You will also need

- ★ 10", 8", and 6" (3 total) sturdy cardboard rounds covered in aluminum foil
- ★ 8 wooden craft sticks
- ★ 10", 8", and 6" cake tier
- ★ Cake stand
- ★ Large decorating coupler
- ★ Metal decorating tips (#21 and #67)
- ★ Decorating bag

Directions

- Prepare two 10" round pans, two 8" round pans, and two 6" round pans by greasing the bottoms and sides and then dusting with flour. Preheat your oven's temperature to 325 degrees F. Depending on your oven's capacity, you might need to work in batches, baking three cake layers first and then finishing the other three. If you would like to do half of the cakes one day and then the other half the next, simply cut the amounts in half for the cake, wrap the baked layers in plastic wrap, and store in the refrigerator until the following day.

- To prepare the crystallized pansies, beat the powdered sugar, meringue powder and water at medium speed in a large bowl. Beat for about 5 minutes or until the mixture becomes creamy. Use a small new paintbrush to brush the creamed mixture onto the petals and leaves of the pansies. Sprinkle the flowers and leaves with the superfine sugar and allow them to set for 24 hours.

- In a very large bowl use an electric mixer to beat the softened butter until creamy. Begin to add the sugar to the butter, working in small batches and beating until well incorporated. While still beating, add the eggs one at a time. Then mix in the flour one cup at a time, alternating with a ¼ cup of the milk. Beat the batter on low speed; mix in the vanilla and orange extracts.

- Divide the batter among the cake pans, putting 5 cups into each 10" pan, 3 cups into each 8" pan, and 2 cups into each 6" pan. Smooth the tops of each with the back of a slightly damp wooden spoon.

- Place the cakes in the preheated oven. Because the cakes vary in size they will bake at different times so it is important to keep a close eye on them and use a toothpick to be sure they are baked completely. On average, the 10" cakes will bake for 40 to 45 minutes, the 8" for 35 to 40, and the 6" for 30 to 35.

- Once the cakes have finished baking, allow them to cool in their pans on cooling racks for 10 minutes. Use a small knife to carefully loosen the cakes from the side of the pans, invert the cakes, and cool completely on the wire racks. If you are not immediately frosting and assembling the cake, wrap in plastic wrap and keep in the refrigerator for up to 24 hours. Alternately you can freeze the cakes in plastic wrap for up to 1 month.

- To assemble the cake, use a serrated knife to slice off the domed top of each cake layer. Use a pastry brush to brush the top of each cake with orange liqueur.

- Make the frosting by combining the butter and cream cheese in a large bowl. Beat the butter and cream cheese together with an electric mixer on medium speed. Once the mixture becomes creamy, slowly add in the powdered sugar and almond liqueur. The final frosting should be smooth and slightly glossy.

- Begin assembling the 10" layer by spreading a thin layer of the frosting on one side of the prepared cardboard round. Place one of the 10" layers on top of the frosted round. Frost the top of this layer with a generous amount of the orange preserves, leaving space to create a 1" border around the edge. Place the second 10" layer on top.

- Use kitchen scissors to cut the wooden craft sticks to match the height of the 10" tier. Insert the sticks into the tier vertically, ensuring that they are evenly spaced and at the same height as the top tier. Frost the top and sides of the cake, using a wet metal spatula to create a smooth look.

- Follow the above procedure with the 8" and 6" layers, leaving the craft sticks out of the 6" layer. Place the 8" tier in the middle of the 10" tier and then place the 6" in the middle of the 8".

- Decorate the assembled cake by piping the top borders with the #21 tip and the bottom borders with the #67 tip. Use the #21 tip again to pipe a second border just overlapping the bottom border created with the #67. Use a small amount of frosting to attach the crystallized pansies and leaves to the cake as desired.

# Mille Crepes

1834

Lady Mendl's Tea Salon in New York is known for its five-course English tea, its charming ambience, and each table's sugar art handcrafted by the famous food artist Reva Paul. But what guests look forward to most is the fourth course. After delighting in freshly baked scones served with Devonshire cream and preserves, the Mille Crepes is presented. A twenty-layer crepe cake elegantly stuffed with French pastry cream, the Mille Crepes has become so popular that Lady Mendl's now ships them around the United States via their popular New York and Los Angeles boutiques, Lady M Confections.

The New York tea salon opened its doors in 1994, but the brownstone that it calls home was built on the corner of 17th and Irving Place in 1834. Originally the building was home to three families, but over time it transitioned into a men's club, a speak easy, a beauty parlor, and a day spa, before being renovated into the Inn that it is today. This historic past creates an incomparable atmosphere at Lady Mendl's, one that transforms the impressive Mille Crepes cake into the perfect symbol of America's ability to seamlessly blend cultures with the flair of the entrepreneurial spirit.

## MILLE MAPLE CREPES CAKE
*Serves 16*

### Ingredients

- ★ 4 tablespoons unsalted butter, melted and cooled + additional for the pan
- ★ 4 large brown eggs, fresh
- ★ 1 cup bread flour
- ★ 1 cup whole milk
- ★ ¼ cup pure maple syrup, grade B
- ★ ¼ teaspoon sea salt

### For the cream

- ★ 1 ½ cups whole milk
- ★ 3 large brown eggs, fresh
- ★ ½ cup pure maple syrup, grade B
- ★ ¼ cup cornstarch
- ★ 1 ½ tablespoons Scotch whiskey
- ★ ½ cup whipping cream
- ★ ¾ tablespoon confectioner's sugar

### To top

- ★ 3 tablespoons granulated sugar

### You will also need

- ★ A kitchen torch

### Directions

- In a blender emulsify the melted butter and eggs. Pour in the flour, milk, maple syrup and salt and continue blending until they are smooth. Allow the batter to cool overnight in the refrigerator or 6 to 8 hours.

- Set the oven's surface temperature to medium low heat and heat a 9" heavy bottomed, non-stick pan until it is hot. Coat the pan with a layer of butter, wiping out the excess with a paper towel so that there are not any pools. Carefully measure out two tablespoons of the refrigerated batter and place in the center of the hot pan. Working quickly, swirl the batter until it spreads to the size of the pan. If the crepe batter will not spread out to the sides, your pan is too hot. If this happens, remove the pan from the heat for several seconds before adding the batter and placing back on the oven top.

- You will know your crepe is ready to flip when the top of it does not look wet. Use a spatula to lift the corner and then, using your fingers to help, flip the crepe being careful not to burn yourself on the hot pan. Cook the crepe for 20 seconds on the second side, just long enough to be sure that it is cooked thorough. Place the cooked crepe on a plate (you will stack them one on top of another as you finish).

- Continue making the remaining crepes as detailed above. Don't re-butter the pan unless the crepes begin to stick when flipped. After all of the crepes have been made, keep them stacked on top of each other, but allow them to cool while you make the cream for the filling.

- Combine the milk, eggs, syrup, and cornstarch in a blender and process until smooth. Using a heavy bottomed pot, pour the blended mixture in and heat over medium low (160 degrees F if using a candy thermometer). Stir the mixture constantly until it thickens. As soon as it thickens, take the filling off the heat and add the Scotch, stirring until well combined. Allow the filling to cool.

- In a bowl beat the whipping cream with an electric mixer until fluffy. Add the confectioner's sugar in batches, beating until peaks form. Once you begin to see peaks holding be sure to stop or the fat will begin to separate out of the cream. Use a spatula to fold this into the cooled filling.

- To assemble the cake, place a crepe (be sure not to use your best one as this will be the top) on a cake plate. Spread a layer of the filling (about as thick as the crepe itself) on top. Continue stacking the layers and filling until all of the crepes have been used – don't worry if all of the filling is used; trying to used all of the filling might result in a cake that is extremely difficult to cut.

- After finishing assembling the cake place it in the refrigerator overnight (or at least 4 hours). This is important because the filling will add moisture to the crepe layers.

- Before serving the cake, sprinkle the top with the granulated sugar and use a kitchen torch to brulee it. Be sure to brulee the sugar quickly since taking too long will start to melt the filling in between the layers. Slice and enjoy immediately.

# Strawberry Short

1850

While shortcake has been around since the sixteenth century, bibliophiles noting its presence in Shakespeare's play The Merry Wives of Windsor, the tradition of adding strawberries and cream to shortcake is deemed an American creation. By 1850 strawberry shortcake had become a popular party staple in the United States, often made as a tribute to the upcoming summer season. "Strawberry Fever", which refers to the increasing demand for strawberries in all areas of the United States with the dawn of the transcontinental railroad, undoubtedly helped to make this dessert even more popular. In 1893 Harper's Magazine even published the now famous line, "They give you good eating, strawberries and short-cake – Ohh My!"

Strawberry shortcake was originally made baking homemade pastry (a biscuit or scone type of creation) and then creating a sandwich with fresh cream and strawberries. Today many people make strawberry shortcake using the pre-made sponge cups often found in the grocery store near the strawberries when they are in season. And although this method still creates a dessert worth indulging in, absolutely nothing can compare with the original homemade strawberry shortcake – it is this method that made the dessert the American classic it is today!

## CLASSIC STRAWBERRY SHORTCAKE
*Serves 4*

### Ingredients

- ★ 4 cups fresh strawberries, washed, hulled, and sliced
- ★ 5 tablespoons sugar

### For the shortcake

- ★ 1½ cups flour
- ★ 1 ½ teaspoons baking powder
- ★ 4 tablespoons sugar
- ★ 1/3 cup cold unsalted butter, sliced
- ★ ½ cup cold milk
- ★ ¾ teaspoon vanilla extract

### For the filling

- ★ Homemade whipped cream, for filling

### Directions

- Set your oven's temperature to 425 degrees F. Combine the strawberries and sugar together in a medium size bowl and set aside.

- To prepare the shortcakes, combine the flour, baking powder, and sugar together in a large bowl with a whisk. Cut the butter in using a pastry blender until the mixture resembles coarse crumbs. Pour in the milk and vanilla and stir to combine.

- Divide the shortcake mixture into 4 even parts and drop onto an ungreased baking sheet. Place the shortcakes in the preheated oven and bake for about 12 minutes or until the cakes become golden brown on top. Once done allow them to cool on a wire rack.

- To serve, split each cake in half (like a biscuit) and top with ¼ of the strawberry mixture (with a lot of juice) and whipped cream. Place the top of the cake back on. Repeat with the other cakes until you have 4 homemade strawberry shortcakes ready for indulging.

★ ★ ★ ★ ★ ★ ★ ★ ★ ★

# SINGER PATENTS THE SEWING MACHINE
## 1851

★ ★ ★ ★ ★ ★ ★ ★ ★ ★

# Minnehaha

1855

Henry Wadsworth Longfellow was born in Portland Maine in 1807 to Stephen Longfellow and Zilpah Wadsworth Longfellow. He was the second of eight children. Fluent in Latin and studious in nature, by age thirteen Longfellow had published his first poem, *The Battle of Lovell's Pond*. Today he is most well remembered as a poet, although Longfellow was also an educator and professor at Bowdoin and Harvard. Some of his most popular works include *Paul Revere's Ride*, *Evangeline*, and the American classic, *The Song of Hiawatha*.

In *The Song of Hiawatha,* Longfellow writes about a princess called Minnehaha, which can be translated as "laughing water" or "waterfall" in its native Dakota. While it is unclear who made the first Minnehaha cake or why the particular ingredients were selected, there is no doubt that this tempting layered cake is an homage to Longfellow's fictional princess and Hiawatha's famous lover.

## THE MINNEHAHA CAKE
*Serves 16*

### Ingredients
- ★ 1 cup whole milk, at room temperature
- ★ 6 egg whites, at room temperature
- ★ 2¼ teaspoons vanilla extract
- ★ 2 ¼ cups cake flour

★ 1 ½ cups + 3 tablespoons granulated sugar
★ 3¾ teaspoons baking powder
★ ¾ teaspoons salt
★ 12 tablespoons unsalted butter, softened and cooled

## For the frosting

★ 2 ½ cups packed dark brown sugar
★ 16 tablespoons unsalted butter, softened and cooled
★ 2/3 cup heavy cream

## For the filling

★ 1 ¼ cups sliced almonds
★ 2/3 cup raisins

## Directions

- Preheat your oven's temperature to 350 degrees F. Prepare three 8" round cake pans by greasing and flouring; set aside.

- Begin preparing the cakes by combining the milk, egg whites, and vanilla in a bowl.

- In a large bowl combine the flour, sugar, baking powder and salt. Beat on low speed with an electric mixer until all of the ingredients have been well combined. Beat in the butter, mixing until moist crumbs form and the mixture looks uniform. Pour in half of the milk mixture. Beat on medium speed for 90 seconds or until smooth. Continue mixing as you add the rest of the milk mixture; beat for another 30 seconds.

- Divide the batter among the 3 prepared pans, smoothing the tops with a slightly wet spatula. Bake the cakes in the preheated oven for about 25 minutes or until a toothpick inserted into the center of the cake comes out clean. Halfway through baking turn the pans to ensure even baking. Allow the cakes to cool in the pans for a few minutes before running a small knife along the sides to loosen the cakes from the pans. Turn the cakes onto wire racks and allow them to cool completely before assembling the cake, about 2 hours.

- While the cakes are cooling make the frosting. In a saucepan combine the sugar, 10 tablespoons of the butter, and the cream. Heat over medium heat and bring to a boil, stirring every few minutes. Use a candy thermometer to bring the mixture to 240 degrees F. At this point the mixture should look very thick. Pour the mixture into a large bowl and beat with an electric mixer on medium speed (using a paddle attachment if available). Once the mixture has cooled to room temperature, mix in the rest of the butter, working 1 tablespoon at a time.

- To create the filling, place ¾ cup almonds, the raisins, and 1 cup of the just-made frosting in a food processor. Process the mixture until the almonds and raisins are ground.

- To assemble the cake place the bottom layer on a cake platter. Spread the top of this layer with half of the filling. Place the second layer on top and spread the remaining half of the filling into a smooth and even layer. Place the third layer on top and frost the sides and top with the frosting. Use the leftover almonds to decorate the bottom edge of the cake.

# Boston Cream

## 1856

In 1856 the now famous Parker House opened its doors in the heart of Boston. Now known as the Omni Parker House, Parker's Restaurant's chef, the Frenchman M. Sanzian, is credited with inventing the popular American dessert, the Boston Cream Pie. Word quickly spread about the dessert, everyone raving about one thing in particular: the chocolate icing. Although called a pie it is in reality a two-layer cake filled with cream. In 1958 the cake's popularity had grown the point the Betty Crocker worked with the Parker House to create a boxed mix that was sold nationally in grocery chains until the 1990's. Despite the competition by Toll House Cookies and Fig Newton, The Boston Cream Pie remains Massachusetts' official state dessert.

## SALEM MEETS BOSTON CREAM PIE
*Serves 12*

### Ingredients

- ★ ½ cup unsalted butter, softened
- ★ 1 cup granulated sugar
- ★ 3 fresh egg yolks
- ★ 1 ½ teaspoons pure vanilla extract
- ★ ¾ cup milk
- ★ 2 cups + 1 tablespoon cake flour
- ★ 2 teaspoons baking powder
- ★ 1/8 teaspoon salt

For the filling
- ★ ½ cup granulated sugar
- ★ 4 fresh egg yolks
- ★ 6 ½ tablespoons cake flour
- ★ 1½ cups milk
- ★ 2¼ teaspoons vanilla extract

For the frosting
- ★ 4 ounces semisweet chocolate, chopped
- ★ ½ cup heavy cream
- ★ 1 tablespoon unsalted butter

Directions
- Set your oven's temperature to 375 degrees F. Grease two 8" round cake pans and line with parchment paper. Set aside.
- Begin by making the cake. In a large bowl, combine the sugar and butter and beat until well combined. Add the egg yolks and continue beating until light and creamy. Use a spatula to scrape the sides before adding in the milk and beating to combine.
- In a small bowl combine the flour, baking powder, and salt. Use a whisk to combine them together. Add this to the butter mixture in the large bowl. Use the electric mixer to beat on medium-high for 30 seconds. Once the batter has formed (it should be thick) and no dry ingredients are visible (be sure to look at the bottom of the bowl!), divide it between your two prepared pans. Use a slightly wet spatula or spoon to spread the batter smooth.
- Place the cakes in the preheated oven and bake for about 20 minutes or until a toothpick inserted into the center of the cake comes out clean. The cakes should be a light golden brown on top and firm to the touch. Allow the cakes to cool in the pans for 10 minutes. Use a small knife to loosen the sides of the cakes from the pans and invert onto a wire rack to finish cooling – remove the parchment paper from the bottom.
- To make the custard filling, add a few inches of water to the bottom of a medium size pot. Place the pot over high heat and bring to a boil.
- Meanwhile, in a heatproof bowl, combine the sugar and yolks and whisk until combined. Add in the flour and whisk again. Then add in the milk and vanilla; whisk. Reduce the heat under the pot of boiling water to low. Set the heatproof bowl over the pot of water to heat. Stir the mixture with a whisk for about 5 minutes or until the filling begins to thicken into a custard. The filling needs to be very thick when it is done. To check this, place a spoon in the custard. If it coats the back of the spoon it is done. Remove the finished filling from the heat and allow it to cool at room temperature for 10 minutes. Place the filling in the refrigerator and allow it to cool completely.

- While the filling cools you can make the frosting. Fill the bottom of a medium size pot with 3" of water (or use the same pot you just used to heat the filling), heat over high until boiling.

- Place the chopped chocolate in a large heatproof bowl; add the cream. Reduce the heat under the boiling pot of water to low and set the heatproof bowl on top of the pot of water. Add the butter to the chocolate and cream and whisk until the chocolate has melted completely and the frosting looks smooth and glossy. Place the bowl of frosting on the counter to cool and thicken. Be cautious if you place it in the refrigerator as it can harden into fudge very quickly.

- To assemble the cake, use a serrated knife to remove the edges of the cake and the domed tops. If too much of the cake breaks off when cutting, don't stress because the filling will help to hold it together. Just use the broken cake as the bottom layer if necessary. Place the first layer on a serving platter and spoon the filling on top. Use a spatula to spread the filling into an even layer. Place the second cake on top. Frost the top of the second layer and the sides of the cake with the frosting.

- To be sure the cake doesn't slide apart while cooling, use a few toothpicks inserted into the top layer and through the second. Allow the cake to cool for another couple hours before slicing and serving (be sure to remove the toothpicks first!)

★ ★ ★ ★ ★ ★ ★ ★ ★ ★

CIVIL WAR BEGINS IN AMERICA
1861

PRESIDENT LINCOLN FREES SLAVES WITH
EMANCIPATION PROCLAMATION
1863

★ ★ ★ ★ ★ ★ ★ ★ ★ ★

# Baked Alaska

1867

In 1867 the Czar of Russia, Alexander II, was facing a national economic crisis. In order to try to diminish the effects of his collapsing royal treasury, Czar Alexander decided to offer the United States a huge opportunity, to buy his "frozen frontier", now known as Alaska. For the unbelievable price of just $7 million (a few cents per each acre), the United States' Secretary of State William Seward purchased what would (nearly a century later) become the 49th state. The acquisition wasn't overwhelmingly popular and the controversy made headlines for months, with many Americans agreeing with Horace Greeley's statement, "The country would not be worth taking as a gift."

At the same time as the frozen frontier debacle, a talented French chef was turning heads at New York City's Delmonico's restaurant. His name was Charles Ranhofer and at only 26 he had become a marketing genius. Knowing to take advantage of headlines in order to sell his dishes, his fancy dessert piled high with frozen meringue transformed from the French classic "Omelette Norvegienne" to the attention grabbing "Baked Alaska".

Was it frozen? Hot? The intrigue sent droves of Americans to Delmonico's in the 1860's and undoubtedly created an American classic, one which may have been delicious enough to change stubborn Americans' opinion on the recently purchased land up north.

## THE GILDED AGE'S BAKED ALASKA
*Serves 8*

### Ingredients

- ★ 4 cups flour
- ★ 3 cups sugar
- ★ 2 cups softened butter
- ★ ¾ cup whole milk
- ★ 6 large brown eggs
- ★ 2½ teaspoons vanilla extract
- ★ 2 tablespoons brandy
- ★ 2 ½ pints strawberry ice cream, softened slightly

### For the topping

- ★ 3 large egg whites, at room temperature
- ★ ¼ teaspoon cream of tartar
- ★ ¾ cup confectioner's sugar

### Directions

- Set your oven's temperature to 325 degrees F. Prepare a 10" tube pan by greasing the bottom and sides and then dusting with flour.

- In a large bowl combine all of the ingredients. Use an electric mixer on low speed to beat the mixture for 1 minute. Use a spatula to scrape the sides and then beat the mixture for another 2 minutes, this time on medium speed. Pour the mixture into the prepared pan and bake in the preheated oven for 90 minutes or until a toothpick inserted into the center of the cake comes out clean.

- When finished baking, place the cake (still in the pan) on a cooling rack for ten minutes. Carefully invert the pan on the cooling rack, removing the cake. Allow the cake to cool for at least an hour.

- Line a 2-quart bowl with aluminum foil, allowing several inches to hang over the edges to make removing the cake easier. Grease the aluminum foil. Slice the cooled cake into half-inch slices. Line the prepared bowl with the slices, pressing firmly to create a "cake bowl". Allow the slices to overlap as much as necessary so that no foil is visible when you are finished. There should be some cake left for the top of the cake later.

- Brush the cake with the brandy. (Note: since the cake will not be baked the alcohol will remain both alcoholic and strong. Use sparingly or leave out completely if necessary.)

- Begin scooping the ice cream into the "cake bowl", filling it completely and avoiding as many air pockets as possible. Smooth the top of the ice cream so that it is flat. Place cake slices on top of the ice cream, filling in the corners so that there are not any gaps. When finished, the ice cream should no longer be visible.

- Fold the aluminum foil edges over the top of the cake, using more foil if necessary to cover the cake completely. Place the cake in the freezer for at least 2 hours. The cake can be kept in the freezer for up to 7 days if needed.

- Before serving the cake, prepare the meringue topping. Preheat your oven's temperature to 450 degrees F. Position the rack in your oven to the lowest level possible so that there is plenty of room.

- In a mixing bowl, beat the egg whites with an electric mixer on medium speed. Once they begin to look frothy add the cream of tartar and 1 tablespoon of the confectioner's sugar. Adjust the speed to high and continue adding in the remaining confectioner's sugar 1 tablespoon at a time until it is all gone. Keep beating on high until stiff peaks form.

- Take the cake out of the freezer and remove any aluminum foil loose on top. Use the hanging edges of foil to remove the cake out of the bowl. Turn the cake upside down and place it on a baking sheet. Any cracks or breaks in the cake from removing it from the bowl (it happens!) will be hidden by the meringue so don't worry.

- As quickly as possible, frost the cake with meringue. Create a smooth layer first, covering the cake completely and then swirl the rest of the meringue on to create a "wispy" type of look. The thicker the meringue layer is the better. Set the cake in the preheated oven for 3 to 4 minutes or until the meringue begins to turn golden brown.

- When finished transfer the cake to a serving platter and serve immediately.

# King

★ ★ ★ ★ ★ ★ ★ ★ ★ ★

1870

New Orleans is known for many things, great music, amazing food, rich culture, but what they are most certainly known for best is their large, sometimes raunchy but always rowdy, Mardi Gras celebration. Known as Epiphany, Twelfth Night, or King's Day, January 6th marks the beginning of the Mardi Gras season, coinciding with the day the Magi brought gifts to the newly born Jesus. The celebration in New Orleans is believed to have begun in the 1870's, with their traditions stemming from the festivities already engrained in Europe's culture.

The King Cake is an integral part of the Mardi Gras festivities, both in New Orleans and around the world. The cake is traditionally baked to honor the three kings and its shape, an oval, meant to symbolize the union of faiths. The colors of Mardi Gras, purple, yellow, and green make a bright appearance on the cake representing justice, power, and faith. Before 1870 a seed was hidden in the cake, the one to find it crowned the "King of the Feast". By 1870 the seed tradition has morphed into more literal symbolism, hiding a small baby figurine in the cake to represent baby Jesus. Whoever finds the baby is supposedly showered with good luck for the year, although, depending on the person's enjoyment of baking, may not be completely accurate as that person is usually responsible for baking the King Cake for next year's festivities.

## CINNAMON SUGAR FILLED KING CAKE
*Serves 16*

### Ingredients

- ★ ½ cup unsalted butter, melted
- ★ 2/3 cup evaporated milk
- ★ ¾ teaspoon granulated sugar + 1 teaspoon
- ★ 1 teaspoon salt
- ★ ¼ cup lukewarm water
- ★ 2 packages active dry yeast (1/4 ounce each)
- ★ 3 eggs
- ★ 1 lemon, for the zest
- ★ 6 cups all-purpose flour
- ★ 4 tablespoons unsalted butter, melted
- ★ 1 egg white
- ★ 1 tablespoon water

### For the filling

- ★ ½ cup granulated sugar
- ★ 1 teaspoon ground cinnamon

### For the icing

- ★ 2 cups confectioner's sugar
- ★ 2 tablespoons whole milk

### For the Mardi Gras fun

- ★ ¾ cups granulated sugar
- ★ Food coloring, yellow, green, red, and blue

### Directions

- In a medium size bowl combine the ½ cup of melted butter, the evaporated milk, ¾ cup of the sugar and the salt. The butter should be hot enough that as you stir the sugar dissolves. Once this happens, allow the mixture to cool.

- In a small bowl combine the yeast, water, and the final teaspoon of sugar. The yeast should dissolve when gently stirred. Let the mixture stand for 10 minutes until it gets foamy. Pour this into the cooled butter mixture, add the eggs and lemon zest, and whisk until well combined.

- Working in batches, begin to whisk the flour into the mixture. Once the mixture gets too thick to whisk, use a wooden spoon to add the remaining flour and create dough. Lightly dust a work surface with flour and begin to knead the dough until it becomes elastic and smooth. Lightly oil a large bowl and place the dough in it. Turn the dough so that all sides get coated and then cover the bowl with a clean towel. Allow the dough to rise for about an hour or until it has doubled in size.

- Meanwhile prepare the cinnamon sugar filling by combining both in a small dish until the color is uniform.

- Prepare a baking sheet by lightly coating with oil and set aside.

- When the dough has doubled, punch down and divide in half. Use a rolling pin to make each half into a 10x15" rectangle. Use a pastry brush to brush the top of each rectangle with the 4 tablespoons of melted butter. Divide the cinnamon sugar mixture in half and sprinkle evenly on top of each buttered rectangle. Starting on the long edge, roll the dough up tightly and seal the seam with a touch of water. Do the same with the other piece of dough. Then wind both of the rolls together so that you have one thick piece of rolled dough. Place this on the prepared baking sheet and bring the ends together to form an oval. Place a towel over the dough and allow it to rise for another hour or until it has double in size.

- Set your oven's temperature to 350 degrees F.

- In a small bowl combine the egg white with the tablespoon of water. Use this mixture to brush the top of the risen dough. Place the cake in the preheated oven and bake for 30 to 35 minutes or until the top is golden brown. When the cake has finished baking take off the pan and let cool on a wire rack for 5 to 10 minutes.

- As the cake bakes prepare the icing by whisking together the sugar and milk in a small bowl, adding more sugar or milk as necessary to get the perfect consistency – thin enough to drizzle but not so thin that it won't stick to the cake.

- To dye your sugar for decorating, put ¼ cup of sugar into 3 small cups. Put a drop of yellow coloring in one, a drop of green in the next, and a drop of red and blue in the last to make purple. Use your fingertips to mix the sugar and dye together, adding more coloring if necessary.

- Once the cake has cooled drizzle the top and sides with the icing and sprinkle with the dyed sugar. Slice the cake to serve. (And hide the baby Jesus if you like – just be sure to tell your guests if you do!)

# Ice Cream

1871

The simple ice cream cake actually has a fairly complicated history. It can be simplified (which is exactly what is being done here) by defining "ice cream" as the creamy, frozen dessert we know it as today. It wasn't until the 17th century that ice cream was invented, but it really didn't gain popularity until a century later. Taking a cue from the Renaissance treat the trifle, frozen ice cream began to be shaped into fancy molds and sometimes covered with chocolate; this is called a bombe. The Victorians began to line the ice cream mold with biscuits or sponge cakes before adding the ice cream. Most historians consider this the very first "ice cream cake".

Although there is a good chance that many Americans were making the Victorian type of ice cream cake, an actual recipe for this type of cake didn't appear until 1871 when it was published in *Mrs. Porter's New Southern Cookery Book*.

## CHOCOLATE MALTED ICE CREAM CAKE WITH CHERRIES
*Serves 16*

### Ingredients
- ★ ¾ cup Dutch cocoa powder
- ★ 1¼ cups all-purpose flour
- ★ ¼ teaspoon salt
- ★ 8 ounces semisweet chocolate, chopped

- ★ 12 tablespoons unsalted butter + 1 tablespoon
- ★ 4 large brown eggs
- ★ 1 ½ cups sugar
- ★ 1 ½ teaspoons vanilla extract
- ★ 1 cup buttermilk
- ★ ½ teaspoon baking soda

For the filling

- ★ 1½ cups whipping cream, cold
- ★ ¼ cup + 2 ½ tablespoons malted milk powder
- ★ ¾ gallon vanilla ice cream, softened

For the frosting

- ★ 1 ¼ cup whipping cream
- ★ 4 tablespoons Dutch cocoa powder
- ★ 2 tablespoons malted milk powder
- ★ 16 maraschino cherries, pits removed

Directions

- Preheat your oven to 325 degrees F. Grease a 9x13" pan with the tablespoon of butter and set aside.

- In a medium bowl sift together the cocoa powder, flour, and salt. In another bowl melt the chocolate and butter together until smooth. In a third medium-size bowl combine the eggs, sugar, and vanilla; whisk. Add the chocolate mixture to the egg mixture and whisk. In another bowl mix together the buttermilk and baking soda and then pour into the chocolate mixture, whisking to combine. Add the dry ingredients and whisk until the batter becomes smooth.

- Pour the batter into the prepared pan and bake in the preheated oven for about 40 minutes or until a toothpick inserted into the center of the cake comes out clean. Allow the cake to cool on a wire rack for an hour.

- Slice the cake into small slices and divide into three even piles; set aside. Prepare a 10" tube pan with grease and press 1/3 of the cake slices into the bottom with your fingertips.

- In a medium bowl combine ½ cup of whipping cream and ¼ cup of malted milk powder and whisk. Let the mixture stand for 4 to 5 minutes and then whisk again to thicken. Add this mixture to the softened ice cream, stirring to combine. Spread half of the ice cream mixture on top of the first cake layer, smoothing with a spatula. Press another 1/3 of the cake slices on top of the ice cream and then cover with the remaining half of the ice cream. Use the last 1/3 of cake slices to cover the final ice cream layer. Cover the finished cake with plastic wrap and set in the freezer for at least 4 hours. The cake can stay in the freezer for up to 5 days if necessary.

- To frost the cake, turn the pan upside down on a serving platter. In a mixing bowl combine the whipping cream, cocoa powder, and malted milk powder. Beat the mixture with an electric mixer until it thickens and holds stiff peaks. Frost the top and sides of the cake with the chocolate malt frosting. Before serving, place the cherries along the edges of the cake, spaced evenly so that each slice will get one cherry.

- Enjoy!

# Birthday

1871

According to historians Americans have the Germans to thank for the delicious and time-honored tradition of birthday cake, specifically the birthday cake *with* candles representing the person's age. The earliest record of a cake with candles presented at someone's birthday celebration is in 1746 at Count Ludwig von Zinzendorf of Marienborn's party in which one guest noted, "There was a Cake as large as any Oven could be found to bake it, and Holes made in the Cake according to the Years of the Person's Age, every one having a Candle stuck into it, and one in the Middle."

From its German heritage, the birthday cake spread throughout Europe during the 18th and early 19th century. And although cakes were baked in America for birthday celebrations, the tradition of putting candles on the cake didn't catch on quickly. It was thanks to publications, such as the Ladies Repository, which highlighted Germany's fun tradition, that we get to enjoy what is considered by most a mandate for birthdays. In 1871 the Ladies Repository published an article in the United States describing the ideal birthday celebration in which they write, "The huge, decorated, birthday cake is place in the center-table, and around it are ranged lighted candles, graduate in length and number by the age of the child."

Where exactly the tradition began of blowing out the candles for good luck is another story. Tracing this history takes us back to Switzerland in 1881 when researchers began documenting Swiss superstitions, one of which stated that "a birthday cake must have lighted candles arranged around it, one candle for each year of life. Before the cake is eaten the person whose birthday it is should blow out the candles one after another. A completely different approach to blowing out candles was documented around the same in New York in the Watertown Daily News, which depicts a ten-year old with a birthday cake at a party. His cake has ten candles although only nine are lit, the tenth representing the year that is just beginning. Rather than the birthday boy blowing out his candles, he selects nine friends to do the honor for him, each making a wish (spoken out loud) for the birthday boy before blowing it out.

In 1909, the idea of keeping the wish secret began to spread via New York's Correct Social Usage book. Around this time, children's magazines in the United States began writing about the birthday boy or girl blowing out their own candles, describing it as a "beautiful part" of the celebration. Sometime later in the 20th century the now popular idea of blowing out all the candles at once, and doing it in a single breath to make the wish come true, took hold.

## DOMINIC'S CHOCOLATE BIRTHDAY CAKE WITH SOUR CREAM FROSTING
*Serves 16*

### Ingredients

- ★ ¾ cup unsalted butter, softened
- ★ 3 eggs
- ★ 2 cups all-purpose flour
- ★ ¾ cup unsweetened cocoa powder
- ★ 1 teaspoon baking soda
- ★ ¾ teaspoon baking powder
- ★ ½ teaspoon salt
- ★ 2 cups sugar
- ★ 2 teaspoons vanilla
- ★ 1 ½ cups skim milk

### For the frosting

- ★ 2 cups semisweet chocolate chips
- ★ ½ cup unsalted butter
- ★ 8 ounces sour cream
- ★ 4 ½ cups powdered sugar, sifted

### Directions

- Set the butter and eggs out on the counter and let warm up to room temperature for 30 minutes. Prepare three 8" round cake pans by greasing the bottoms and then lining with waxed paper. Grease and flour the pans again and set aside. Preheat your oven to 350 degrees F.

- Combine the flour, cocoa powder, baking soda, baking powder, and salt in a medium bowl and stir; set aside. In a larger mixing bowl, begin to beat the butter on high speed with an electric mixer. Beat for 30 seconds and then begin to add the sugar ¼ cup at a time, beating on medium speed. Beat for another 2 minutes. Once all of the sugar has been incorporated add the eggs 1 at a time, beating each one in after being added. Add the vanilla and beat.

- Working in batches, alternately add the flour mixture and milk to the creamed butter mixture; beat on low speed after each addition. Once all of the ingredients have been combined turn the electric mixer to high and beat for another 20 seconds. Divide the mixture evenly between the three prepared pans, using a spatula to even out the tops.

- Set the cakes in the preheated oven and bake for 30 to 35 minutes or until a toothpick inserted into the center of the cakes comes out clean. Allow the cakes to cool in their pans for 10 minutes before removing, taking off the waxed paper, and cooling on wire racks.

- While the cakes cool, prepare the frosting. Melt the chocolate and butter in a large saucepan over low heat, stirring constantly. Once completely melted allow the mixture to cool for 5 minutes. Stir in the sour cream and then gradually add in the powdered sugar. Use an electric mixer to beat until it is smooth.

- To assemble the cake place the first layer on a cake platter and frost the top. Repeat with the second and third layers and then frost the sides. Decorate the cake with candles, sprinkles, or whatever else your birthday pal would like and enjoy!

# Cheese

1872

Although New Yorkers will glad take credit for inventing the cheesecake, this popular dessert's history can be traced back to Samos, a Greek island, where anthropologists and historians discovered cheese cake molds. Written documents reveal that these first cheesecakes were served to athletes (possibly the first Olympic athletes in 776 B.C) before events for energy. Cheesecakes were also served at Greek weddings as far back as 230 A.D, which is the same time that the first cheesecake recipe was written by Athenaeus (it is believed that this may very well be the first written recipe ever!)

Cheesecake has made its way across the globe over several centuries, each culture and country putting its own unique mark on the ancient dessert. When cheesecake reached the United States in the early 1800's it was very similar to the European cheesecake, sweet, no strong yeast flavor, but still a far cry from the dessert Americans enjoy today. The invention of the modern cheesecake happened in 1872 when a New York farmer accidentally invented cream cheese while trying to recreate Neufchatel, a popular French cheese. Philadelphia Cream Cheese began delivering its product to American stores in 1875 and continued to do so until 1928 when the Kraft Cheese Company bought them out. At this point New York Style Cheesecake had become incredibly popular, each chef and household putting its own unique spin on it, but no one daring to exclude the ingredient that makes it so tasty: cream cheese.

## CHOCOLATE BROWNIE CHEESECAKE
*Serves 16*

*Makes 2 Individual Cakes*

### Ingredients
- ★ 4 ounces unsweetened chocolate baking squares, melted
- ★ 1 cup unsalted butter, softened
- ★ 2 cups cane sugar
- ★ 4 large brown eggs
- ★ 1 cup all-purpose flour
- ★ 1 teaspoon vanilla extract
- ★ 1 ¼ cup semisweet chocolate chips (about 7 to 8 ounces)
- ★ 32 ounces cream cheese, softened
- ★ 1 ¾ cups cane sugar
- ★ 7 large brown eggs
- ★ 2 teaspoons pure vanilla extract

### For the glaze
- ★ 4 cups semisweet chocolate chips (about 24 ounces)
- ★ 1 cup whipping cream

### Directions
- Grease and flour two 9" round springform pans and set aside. Set your oven's temperature to 325 degrees F.

- In a mixing bowl, combine the butter and 2 cups of sugar and beat on medium speed with an electric mixer until the mixture becomes fluffy. Beat in the eggs one at a time and then add the melted chocolate, beating until the mixture is uniform in color. On low speed, beat in the flour. Mix in the vanilla and chocolate chips. Pour the mixture evenly into both of the prepared pans.

- In a clean mixing bowl, use the electric mixer on medium speed to beat the cream cheese until it becomes smooth in texture. Beat in the 1¾ cups of sugar and then add the 7 eggs one at a time, mixing after each addition. Mix in the vanilla. Evenly divide this mixture on top of the chocolate mixture in the pans, smoothing the tops so that they are even and cover all of the chocolate.

- Set the pans in the preheated oven and bake for 70 to 75 minutes or until the cakes have set. Once finished, allow them to cool on cooling racks completely before topping with the chocolate glaze.

- To prepare the glaze, melt the chocolate chips and then whisk in the whipping cream until the mixture is smooth. Pour the glaze over the top of each cooled cheesecake, using a slightly wet knife to spread evenly.

- If desired, top with fresh fruit, such as strawberries or cherries.

ALEXANDER GRAHAM BELL PATENTS HIS
INVENTION, THE TELEPHONE
1876

# Coffee

## 1876

More like bread than the cake we are familiar with today, the first coffee cakes most likely were created in either Northern or Central Europe during the 17$^{th}$ century. These breads, although different than American coffee cake, still utilized the delicious crumb or streusel topping to sweeten up the post-meal treat. When the idea of coffee cakes arrived in America in the late 19$^{th}$ century, coffee became an actual ingredient, not just an accompaniment. The first record of a coffee-type cake not made with coffee but rather served with coffee (or perhaps dunked right in!) was in 1876 in a Philadelphia newspaper article. It wasn't until 1920 that coffee cake became its own unique genre in American cookbooks.

## SOUR CREAM CHERRY COFFEE CAKE
*Serves 12*

### Ingredients

- ★ ½ cup butter
- ★ 1 cup sugar
- ★ 2 fresh eggs
- ★ 2 cups all-purpose flour
- ★ 1 teaspoon baking powder
- ★ ¼ teaspoon baking soda
- ★ ½ teaspoon salt
- ★ 1 cup low-fat sour cream

For the filling and topping

★ ½ cup sugar
★ 2½ teaspoons ground cinnamon
★ 2¼ teaspoons pure vanilla extract
★ ½ cup chopped fresh cherries (or thawed if frozen), pits removed

Directions

- Preheat your oven to 350 degrees F. Prepare a 9x9" baking pan by greasing and flouring the bottoms and sides; set aside. Prepare the filling and topping mixture by combining all ingredients in a small bowl and mixing until everything is evenly distributed; set aside.

- In a large bowl combine the butter, sugar, and eggs and cream with an electric mixer. In another large bowl, combine the flour, baking powder, baking soda, and salt, stirring to combine. Add this mixture to the creamed mixture and stir to combine. Working in batches, add in the sour cream, stirring after each addition. Divide the batter into the prepared pan and sprinkle with half of the filling and topping mixture. Pour the remaining batter on top and then sprinkle with the rest of the filling and topping mixture.

- Bake the cake in the preheated oven for about 30 minutes or until a toothpick inserted into the center of the cake comes out clean. Allow the cake to cool for 10 minutes before slicing and serving.

# Ambrosia

1877

By definition ambrosia is "a dessert made from fruits, sugar and grated coconut, most popular in the South." It wasn't until the 1870's however that "ambrosia" began to be used in the United States as the name for this type of dessert. Enthusiasts of classic mythology will recognize the name ambrosia since it, along with nectar, was quite literally the food of gods. Supposedly ambrosia, a porridge type of meal comprised of honey, fruit, olive oil, cheese, and barley, was one of the key elements to the gods' immortality; if consumed by mortals, however, ambrosia was fatal.

The first documented American recipe for Ambrosia was published in the 1877 cookbook, Buckeye Cookery. This particular 19th century recipe calls for oranges, pineapple, coconut, and sugar. But like all good American things, people tend to believe that something good can be turned into something great, or in this case delicious. And while things like this don't always work out (Edison would probably like to forget about the cement piano), in the case of taking ambrosia and turning it into cake, things worked out splendidly.

## PINEAPPLE FILLED ORANGE AMBROSIA CAKE
*Serves 12*

### Ingredients
- ★ 1 cup cake flour, sifted
- ★ 1 ½ cups granulated sugar, sifted

★ 12 large egg whites, at room temperature (save 1 egg yolk for the pineapple filling_
★ 1 teaspoon cream of tartar
★ ¼ teaspoon salt
★ 1 ¾ teaspoons pure vanilla extract
★ 1½ teaspoons freshly squeezed lemon juice
★ ½ teaspoon almond extract

For the pineapple filling

★ ¼ cup pineapple juice
★ 2 large eggs + 1 egg yolk
★ ½ cups sugar
★ 2 tablespoons unsalted butter
★ 1/8 teaspoon salt

For the frosting

★ 2 teaspoons vanilla extract
★ 2 tablespoons heavy cream
★ 1/8 tablespoons salt
★ 2½ cups confectioner's sugar
★ 20 tablespoons unsalted butter, softened
★ 1 teaspoon orange zest
★ 2 teaspoons freshly squeezed orange juice

For the decoration

★ 30 ounces mandarin oranges, drained and chopped
★ 2 cups sweetened shredded coconut, toasted
★ 20 ounces pineapple slices, drained and cut in half

Directions

- Preheat your oven to 325 degrees F. Line a 9" tube pan with parchment paper and set aside.

- Combine the flour and ¾ cup of sugar in a small bowl and whisk. In a medium bowl beat the egg whites with an electric mixer on low speed. Once the egg whites begin to look frothy, mix in the cream of tartar and salt on medium speed. Then beat in the remaining ¾ cup of sugar 1 tablespoon at a time. Continue beating until the egg whites begin to hold soft peaks. Beat in the vanilla, lemon juice, and almond extract.

- Place the flour/sugar mixture in a sifter and sift into the egg white mixture a bit at a time. Use a spatula to fold the flour mixture in after each addition. Pour the mixture into the prepared pan and tap on the counter a few times to get rid of any air pockets.

- Bake the cake in the preheated oven for about an hour or until it is golden brown and springy to the touch. Allow the cake to cool for 2 hours in the pan before loosening the sides with a small knife and inverting onto a platter. Remove the parchment paper.

- Prepare the pineapple filling by placing the pineapple juice in a saucepan and heating to a boil over medium heat. In a medium-sized bowl whisk together the eggs, yolk, and sugar; continue whisking as you pour in the hot pineapple juice. Return this mixture to the saucepan and heat, stirring, until it thickens, about 3 minutes. Turn off the heat and add the butter and salt, stirring to combine. Strain this mixture into a small bowl and cover with plastic wrap. Set this in the refrigerator for at least an hour so that it thickens.

- Meanwhile prepare the frosting by placing the butter in a mixing bowl and creaming with an electric mixer on medium-high speed. Adjust the speed to medium-low and beat in the confectioner's sugar and salt. Add in the vanilla and heavy cream and beat for 10 seconds on medium speed. Adjust the speed to medium-high and beat for 4 minutes or until it looks fluffy and light.

- Place 1 cup of the frosting in a separate bowl and stir in the orange zest and orange juice.

- To assemble the cake use a sharp serrated knife to slice the cake horizontally into 4 layers. Set the first layer on a cake platter and top with ½ cup of the orange flavored frosting. Sprinkle the top of the frosting with a thin layer of orange slices. Set the next cake layer on top and frost with the pineapple filling. Place the third cake layer on top and frost with the remaining orange frosting and another thin layer of orange slices. Place the final cake layer on top and frost the top and sides with the plain frosting. Decorate the sides of the cake with the toasted coconut, pineapple slices, and remaining orange slices.

THOMAS EDISON INVENTS THE
INCANDESCENT LIGHT
1879

# Robert E. Lee

1879

The Civil War General, known for his controversial yet methodical military strategy and a venerated Southern hero, would appreciate both the effort required and the flavor produced in this famous cake, whether or not he got to profess his gratitude for this fabulous dessert is unknown. The first written recipe discovered for the Robert E. Lee cake was published in 1879 in the cookbook *Housekeeping In Old Virginia*, nine years after his death. It is of course quite possible that this cake was made for Lee himself, some stories claiming that it was in fact his favorite cake, but only he would know for sure (and, believe me, he would remember this cake if he had it!) Other sources state that this cake was made in honor of the fallen Civil War general, its popularity spreading with his paradoxical legend.

Recipes for this cake vary throughout the South, but almost all combine the two citrus flavors, orange and lemon, since family of Lee confirm that those were indeed his favorite flavors.

## GENERAL ROBERT E. LEE'S LEMON LAYER CAKE
*Serves 12*

### Ingredients
- ★ 1 cup unsalted butter, softened
- ★ 2 cups sugar
- ★ 1 lemon, for the zest
- ★ 1 orange, for the zest

★ 4 large eggs, at room temperature
★ 3 cups cake flour, sifted
★ 2 ½ teaspoons baking powder
★ 1 ¼ teaspoons baking soda
★ 1 teaspoon kosher salt
★ 1 cup buttermilk, warm
★ 1 tablespoon pure vanilla extract

For the filling
★ 2 large eggs, at room temperature
★ 4 large egg yolks, at room temperature
★ 1 1/3 cups sugar
★ 2/3 cup freshly squeezed lemon juice
★ 2 lemons, for the zest
★ 2 oranges, for the zest
★ ¾ cup unsalted butter, cold and chopped

For the frosting
★ 2 cups unsalted butter, softened and chopped
★ 3 tablespoons freshly squeezed lemon juice, strained
★ 2 tablespoons freshly squeezed orange juice, strained
★ 4 large egg whites, at room temperature
★ 1 cup sugar
★ 1/8 teaspoon cream of tartar
★ 1/8 teaspoon kosher salt

Directions

- Before preparing the cake prepare the filling. Start by placing the eggs, egg yolks, sugar, lemon juice, and fruit zests in a saucepan and whisk to combine. Heat the mixture over medium heat, stirring constantly until thick, about 14 minutes. Remove the thickened mixture from the heat and whisk in the butter. Pour the mixture through a strainer and into a small bowl. Cover the bowl with plastic wrap and place in the refrigerator for at least 2 hours. Be sure the plastic wrap touches the filling so that a skin does not form.

- To prepare the cake begin by preheating the oven to 350 degrees F. Grease 3 9" round pans and line with parchment paper; set aside. Place the butter in a mixing bowl and beat with an electric mixer on medium speed for 2 minutes. Beat in the sugar and fruit zests, mixing until the mixture appears fluffy, 4 to 5 minutes. Then add in the eggs 1 at a time, mixing after each one.

- In a separate medium-size bowl combine the flour, baking powder, baking soda, and salt and then whisk to combine. Working in batches, beat this mixture into the creamed egg mixture, alternating with batches of buttermilk and vanilla. Divide this batter evenly among the prepared cake pans, using a spatula to even out the tops. Allow the cakes to bake in the preheated oven for about 25 minutes or until a toothpick inserted into the center of the cake comes out clean. The cakes should cool in their pans for 10 minutes before inverting onto cooling racks and removing the parchment paper. The cakes should be completely cool before frosting them.

- As the cakes cool create the frosting by beating the butter in a mixing bowl on medium speed for 3 minutes. Add the fruit juices and beat for another minute. Transfer this mixture into a small bowl.

- Heat a medium saucepan of water on the oven until simmering. In another mixing bowl combine the egg whites, sugar, cream of tartar, and salt and whisk until well mixed. Place this bowl over the saucepan of simmering water and heat and whisk for 10 minutes or until a candy thermometer reads 140 degrees F. Remove the bowl from the heat and beat with an electric mixer on high speed for about 8 minutes or until it is cool and holding soft peaks. Working in batches, beat in the creamed butter until all is well combined.

- To assemble the cake set the bottom layer on a cake platter. Divide the lemon filling in half and spread onto the top of the first layer. Place the second cake layer on top and spread the second half of the filling on top. Top with the final cake layer and frost the top and sides with the homemade frosting.

★ ★ ★ ★ ★ ★ ★ ★ ★ ★

FRED OTT'S SNEEZE BECOMES THE
FIRST U.S. FILM
1889

★ ★ ★ ★ ★ ★ ★ ★ ★ ★

# Lane

## 1898

Named after its inventor, the Southern gal Emma Rylander Lane, the Lane Cake was originally called "Prize Cake" because of its blue ribbon win at Columbus, Georgia's County Fair. Emma published a cookbook (a self-published cookbook!) in 1898 rightfully titled *Some Good Things To Eat,* which included a recipe for her prize-winning cake, filled with raisins, pecans, and coconut. Originally the cake was considered a difficult feat to make, but now with modern appliances you will find it is actually simpler than most.

## EMMA LANE'S "GOOD" CAKE
*Serves 16*

### Ingredients

- ★ 16 tablespoons unsalted butter + additional for pans
- ★ 3 ½ cups cake flour, sifted
- ★ 4 teaspoons baking powder
- ★ ¼ teaspoon salt
- ★ 2 cups granulated sugar
- ★ 1 ½ teaspoons vanilla extract
- ★ 1 cup 2% milk
- ★ ½ teaspoon cream of tartar
- ★ 8 egg whites, at room temperature

For the filling

- ★ 1 cup sugar
- ★ 8 egg yolks
- ★ ½ cup bourbon
- ★ 8 tablespoons unsalted butter, diced
- ★ 1 cup raisins
- ★ 1 cup chopped pecans
- ★ 1¼ cups grated sweetened coconut
- ★ 1 teaspoon vanilla extract

For the frosting

- ★ 1 ½ cups granulated sugar
- ★ 2 tablespoons light corn syrup
- ★ ¼ teaspoon salt
- ★ 4 egg whites, cold

Directions

- Set your oven's temperature to 350 degrees F. Prepare two 9" round cake pans by greasing and flouring; set aside.

- In a medium bowl, combine the flour, baking powder, and salt together with a whisk and set aside. In a mixing bowl cream together the butter, 1 ½ cups of the sugar, and vanilla with an electric mixer on medium-high speed (use the paddle attachment if available). Once the mixture becomes fluffy, work in batches to alternate adding the flour mixture and milk, mixing after each addition. In a separate large bowl combine the cream of tartar and egg whites; whisk until the mixture holds stiff peaks. Pour this mixture into the cake batter, folding in with a spatula.

- Evenly divide the batter between the prepared pans, smoothing the tops with a spatula. Place the cakes in the preheated oven and bake for about 40 minutes or until a toothpick inserted into the center comes out clean. Allow the cakes to cook in their pans for 30 minutes before inverting on wire racks to cool completely. Once cool, use a sharp serrated knife to cut the layers in half horizontally, making 4 equal layers.

- To prepare the filling combine the sugar and egg yolks in a saucepan over medium heat. Add in the bourbon and butter, whisking to combine. Allow the mixture to come to a simmer as you whisk without stopping. As the mixture heats it should thicken – this should take about 2 minutes. Take the saucepan off the heat and allow it to cool completely. Stir in the remaining filling ingredients and set aside.

- Start to make the frosting by placing the sugar, corn syrup, salt, and egg whites in a mixing bowl. Heat a saucepan of water (just enough to cover the bottom) until it simmers. Once simmering place the mixing bowl on top – the bottom of the mixing bowl should not touch the water. Whisk the mixture as it heats. Once a candy thermometer reads 140 degrees F. remove the mixing bowl from the heat and beat on medium-high speed with an electric mixer until it holds stiff peaks.

- To assemble the cake, place the first layer on a serving platter and top with 1/3 of the filling. Repeat with the next two layers. Place the final cake layer on top and frost the top and sides of the cake. Allow the cake to stand in the refrigerator for at least an hour before serving.

THE WRIGHT BROTHERS ATTEMPT TO
FLY THEIR FIRST AIRPLANE
1903

# Devil's Food

★ ★ ★ ★ ★ ★ ★ ★ ★ ★

1905

Unlike most cakes Americans have come to love, Devil's Food cake is truly an American invention. With more chocolate both in the cake and frosting than a regular chocolate cake, Devil's Food is a sinfully tempting dessert. To get the deeper, darker chocolate color, this specific cake uses extra baking soda and fewer eggs than most traditional cake recipes. The first Devil's Food recipe appeared in the United States in 1905 although many food historians agree that it had been a popular cake on the East Coast and in the South decades before this date.

## DARK DEVIL'S FOOD CAKE
*Serves 12*

### Ingredients
★ 1 ½ cups unsalted butter + additional for pans
★ ¾ cup Dutch cocoa powder + additional for pans
★ ½ cup very hot (near boiling) water
★ 2 ¼ cups granulated sugar
★ 1 tablespoon + 1 teaspoon vanilla extract
★ 4 large eggs, gently whisked
★ 3 cups cake flour, sifted
★ 1 teaspoon baking soda
★ ¼ teaspoon kosher salt
★ 1 cup 2% milk

For the frosting

★ 8 ounces high quality milk chocolate (like Perugina or Lindt), chopped
★ ¼ cup unsalted butter, at room temperature
★ 2/3 cup sour cream
★ 4 teaspoons light corn syrup

Directions

- Preheat your oven's temperature to 350 degrees F. Grease three 8" round cake pans with butter and then line the bottoms with parchment paper. Rather than flour, use cocoa powder to dust the pans and set aside.

- In a medium bowl sift the cocoa powder and then use a whisk to add the hot water; set aside to cool. Once cool whisk in the milk.

- In a medium-size mixing bowl, beat the butter on low speed until it appears fluffy. Add in the sugar, beating on low speed for 4 minutes or until it looks fluffy again. Add the vanilla and beat. Working in small additions, add the eggs, beating after each addition.

- Sift the flour, baking soda, and salt together in a large bowl. Set your electric mixer to low and, working in small batches, alternate adding in the flour mixture and the cocoa/milk mixture, mixing after each addition. Pour your batter evenly into the prepared pans and bake in the preheated oven for about 40 minutes or until a toothpick inserted into the center of the cakes comes out clean. Halfway through baking, rotate the pans to ensure even baking. Once done, allow the cakes to cool in their pans on wire racks for 15 minutes before inverting out of the pans and cooling completely. Remove the parchment paper from the bottoms of the cakes.

- To make the frosting, begin by simmering a saucepan of water over medium-low heat. Place the chocolate in a large heatproof bowl and set over the simmering water. Stir the chocolate until it has melted and appears smooth in texture. Take the bowl off the water and stir in the butter. Once the butter has melted, add in the sour cream and corn syrup, whisking until the mixture is smooth. Before using on the cake, allow the frosting to thicken at room temperature for 15 to 20 minutes.

- To assemble the cake, place the bottom layer on a cake stand and frost the top. Place the second layer on top and repeat. Finish with the final layer and frost the top and sides until all of the cake is covered.

# Lady Baltimore

1906

Whether or not Lady Baltimore herself ate this cake is hard to know, although many who call Maryland their home will ardently argue that of course she did (and then will continue to tell you about the Lord Baltimore cake, one invented by the Lord himself to use up all of the egg yolks his wife was wasting). While the above story can be argued, the fact that the Lady Baltimore cake reached the peak of its fame in 1906 cannot. It was in 1906 that the author Owen Wister gave his famous romance novel the name, *Lady Baltimore*. More than just a title, the cake itself makes a grand appearance in his book, being described as "all soft, and it's in layers, and it has nuts – but I can't write any more about it; my mouth waters too much". Topped with meringue and filled with a fruit and nut filling, this cake lives up to its literary status.

## THE LADY BALTIMORE CAKE
*Serves 12*

### Ingredients

- ★ 3 cups cake flour, sifted
- ★ 4 teaspoons baking powder
- ★ 1/8 teaspoon kosher salt
- ★ 1 1/3 cups milk
- ★ 2 tablespoons vanilla extract

★ ¾ cup vegetable shortening
★ 1 cup + 2 tablespoons granulated sugar
★ 6 large egg whites

For the filling and frosting
★ ½ cup raisins
★ ¼ cup kirsch (or rum if unavailable)
★ 2 cups granulated sugar
★ ½ cup water
★ 4 large egg whites
★ 1/8 teaspoon kosher salt
★ 2 ¼ teaspoons vanilla extract
★ ½ cup finely chopped walnuts
★ ½ cup chopped dried figs

Directions
- Set your oven's temperature to 375 degrees F. Prepare two 8" round cake pans by greasing and lining the bottoms with parchment paper; set aside.

- In a medium-sized bowl, sift the flour, baking powder, and salt. In a small bowl combine the milk and vanilla.

- In a mixing bowl, combine the shortening and 1 cup of the sugar. Use an electric mixer (with the paddle attachment if available) to cream the two together. On low speed, alternate adding in the flour mixture and milk mixture in batches until combined.

- In another mixing bowl, beat the egg whites on low speed until it becomes frothy. With the mixer still running add in the remaining sugar 1 tablespoon at a time. Adjust the speed to high and mix until the mixture holds stiff peaks. Use a spatula to fold half of the egg white mixture into the flour mixture. Then fold in the remaining egg whites.

- Pour the batter evenly into the prepared pans, smoothing the tops. Bake the cakes in the preheated oven for 25 minutes or until a toothpick inserted into the center of the cakes comes out clean. Allow the cakes to cool in their pans for 15 minutes on wire racks. Then take the cakes out of their pans, remove the parchment paper, and cool completely on the wire racks.

- To make the filling and frosting, start by setting the raisins and kirsch in a small bowl. Place the sugar and ½ cup of water in a saucepan and bring to a boil. Use a candy thermometer to watch the temperature of the sugar and water. Remove the saucepan from the heat once it reaches 236 degrees F.

- In a mixing bowl, beat the egg whites until they are frothy. Then add in the salt and beat until the egg whites become stiff. Continue mixing as you add the hot sugar/water mixture. Mix for 3 minutes before adding in the vanilla. This is your frosting.

- Take 1/3 of the frosting and transfer to a medium-size bowl. Drain the raisins from the kirsch and stir in, adding the walnuts and figs. This is your filling.

- To assemble the cake, use a sharp serrated knife to remove the domed tops from the cakes. Place the first layer on a cake stand and spread the filling over the top. Place the second layer, bottom side up, on top and frost the top and sides of the cake.

# Wellesley Fudge

★ ★ ★ ★ ★ ★ ★ ★ ★ ★

1913

Henry and Pauline Durant founded Wellesley, an all girls' college, in 1870. In 1875 the college opened its doors to its first class of women, giving way to its first graduating class, eighteen in total, in 1879. Serious about educating women, Wellesley enforced some strict campus rules, including an early curfew. The college, however, encouraged lady-like hobbies and interests, one of which was the art of candy making. In the late 1800's and early 1900's fudge had become a popular sweet and the girls at Wellesley used it as a way to extend their curfews, hosting "candy-making parties" in their dorms. The name "fudge" is perhaps not a coincidence for this sweet, considering that the girls at the college would use it as a way to cheat the system, most parties really focusing on boys and romances. In 1913, the words "Wellesley" and "fudge" had become well intertwined, with the majority of America understanding, and enjoying, the girls' misleading charade.

## SLIGHTLY NAUGHTY WELLESLEY FUDGE CAKE
*Serves 16*

### Ingredients
- ★ 2½ cups all-purpose flour
- ★ 2 teaspoons baking soda
- ★ 1 teaspoon baking powder
- ★ ½ teaspoon salt
- ★ ¾ cup hot water

★ ½ cup Dutch cocoa powder
★ 16 tablespoons unsalted butter, divided into 16 pieces and softened
★ 2 ¼ cups granulated sugar
★ 2 large eggs, at room temperature
★ 1 cup buttermilk, at room temperature
★ 2 teaspoons pure vanilla extract

For the frosting

★ 1 ½ cups light brown sugar, packed
★ 1 cup evaporated milk
★ 8 tablespoons unsalted butter, divided into 8 pieces and softened
★ ½ teaspoon salt
★ 10 ounces bittersweet chocolate, chopped
★ 1 ¼ teaspoons pure vanilla extract
★ 3 cups confectioner's sugar, sifted

Directions

- Preheat your oven to 350 degrees F. Prepare two 8" square baking pans with grease and flour. Line the bottoms of the pans with parchment paper.

- In a large bowl, stir together the flour, baking soda, baking powder and salt; set aside. In a separate, smaller bowl combine the hot water and cocoa powder, whisking until smooth. Then in a mixing bowl combine the butter and sugar. Beat the two together with an electric mixer on medium-high speed for 5 minutes or until fluffy. One at a time, add the eggs, beating after each addition. Working in batches, add the flour mixture and buttermilk, alternating and mixing after each batch is added until all has been incorporated. Lower the mixer's speed to low and add the cocoa mixture, beating until the consistency is even and the batter is smooth.

- Pour the batter evenly into the two prepared pans, smoothing the tops with a spatula. Bake the cakes in the preheated oven for approximately 28 minutes. To test doneness, insert a toothpick into the center of the cakes. When removed, the toothpick should have a few (not many) crumbs attached. The cakes should cool in their pans for 15 minutes before removing and cooling completely (about 2 hours) on a wire rack. Remove the parchment paper.

- Begin to prepare the frosting by combining the brown sugar, half of the evaporated milk, 4 tablespoons of butter, and the salt in a large saucepan. Place the saucepan over medium heat and cook for 5 to 7 minutes or until small bubbles surface. Decrease the heat to low and bring to a simmer, stirring every few minutes. Once large bubbles surface and the mixture looks thick, transfer it into a large bowl. Then add the remaining half of evaporated milk and the remaining 4 tablespoons of butter, stirring until it cools. Stir in the chocolate and vanilla. Once smooth, whisk in the confectioner's sugar. Allow the frosting to cool for about an hour, stirring every 10 minutes or so.

- To assemble the cake, place the bottom layer on a cake platter. Frost with 1 cup of the frosting and then place the second layer on top. Frost the top and sides of the cake and place in the refrigerator for an hour before slicing and serving.

★ ★ ★ ★ ★ ★ ★ ★ ★ ★

WORLD WAR I BEGINS
1914

UNITED STATES DECLARES WAR AGAINST
GERMANY AND JOINS WORLD WAR I
1917

18TH AMENDMENT IS PASSED PROHIBITING
ALCOHOL AND 19TH AMENDMENT IS PASSED
GIVING WOMEN THE RIGHT TO VOTE
1920

★ ★ ★ ★ ★ ★ ★ ★ ★ ★

# Pineapple Upside Down

★ ★ ★ ★ ★ ★ ★ ★ ★ ★

## 1925

Skillet cakes, which in the mid-1800s were known as "spider cakes" were becoming popular by the 1920s in America thanks to frequent publications both in magazines and cookbooks. Known as a simple yet delicious cake, perfect for utilizing the now common home iron oven, they quickly earned the nickname "upside-down cake" which would eventually replace the traditional name. In 1925 an issue of the publication "American Cookery" suggested adding pineapple to "upside-down cakes" and thus giving thousands Americans the idea for the first Pineapple Upside Down Cake.

## OLD FASHIONED PINEAPPLE UPSIDE DOWN CAKE
*Serves 10*

### Ingredients

- ★ ¼ cup unsalted butter
- ★ 2/3 cup packed dark brown sugar
- ★ 1 (20-ounce) can whole pineapple slices
- ★ 9 maraschino cherries
- ★ 2 large brown eggs, separated
- ★ ¾ cup granulated sugar
- ★ ¾ cup flour
- ★ Pinch of salt
- ★ ½ teaspoon baking powder

Directions

- Preheat your oven's temperature to 325 degrees F.

- In a 9" heavy bottom, ovenproof skillet, melt the butter and remove from heat. Add the brown sugar, spreading it evenly over the bottom of the skillet. Drain the juice from the pineapple, saving ¼ cup of it for later. Decoratively arrange the pineapple slices in a single layer on top of the brown sugar, placing a cherry in the center of each ring.

- In a large mixing bowl beat the egg yolks until they thicken. Working in small batches, beat in the granulated sugar.

- Over low heat, heat the reserved ¼ cup of pineapple juice in a small saucepan. Once warm, add the juice into the egg yolk mixture, beating on low until combined. In a separate bowl stir together the flour, salt, and baking powder; add this mixture to the yolk mixture and beat on low speed until combined.

- In a small bowl beat the egg whites on high until they hold stiff peaks. Fold the egg whites into the batter. Using a large spoon, divide the batter evenly over the pineapple slices. Bake the cake in the preheated oven for 45 minutes. Allow the cake to cool in the skillet for 30 minutes before inverting onto a serving platter. Serve immediately or set in the refrigerator to chill if you would like to serve it cold (both are delicious!)

# Whoopie

★ ★ ★ ★ ★ ★ ★ ★ ★ ★ ★

1925

Giant cake cookies filled with fluffy white cream, the Whoopie Pie is one of Maine's most beloved desserts, its history dating back to the early 20<sup>th</sup> century. Labadie's Bakery in the small town of Lewiston, Maine began selling Whoopie Pies in 1925 with the opening of their first store. That store continues to sell the same delicious (and now famous) Whoopie Pies from their very first location. Before being made famous in Maine, Whoopie Pies were a common treat in the Pennsylvanian Amish culture, a clever usage for extra batter from the day's baking. Supposedly the dessert's name comes from a teacher noting how kids would exclaim "Whoopie" when they were pleasantly surprised at finding the chocolate sandwich in their lunch. It wasn't until 1930, however, that the filling for the Whoopie Pie would forever be changed (for the better) with the invention and concurrent promotion for Marshmallow Fluff.

## MAINE'S MAIN WHOOPIE PIE
*Serves 6*

### Ingredients
★ 2 cups flour
★ ½ cup Dutch cocoa powder
★ 1 teaspoon baking soda
★ ½ teaspoon salt
★ 1 cup light brown sugar, firmly packed
★ 8 tablespoons unsalted butter, softened

★ 1 large egg, at room temperature
★ 1 ¼ teaspoons pure vanilla extract
★ ¾ cup buttermilk

For the filling

★ 12 tablespoons unsalted butter, softened
★ 1 ¼ cups confectioner's sugar
★ 1 ½ teaspoons pure vanilla extra
★ Pinch of salt
★ 2 ½ cups Marshmallow Fluff
★ Confectioner's sugar, for dusting (optional)

Directions

- Preheat your oven to 350 degrees F. Place parchment paper on 2 baking sheets and set aside.

- In a medium-size bowl combine the flour, cocoa powder, baking soda, and salt; whisk. In a separate large bowl, combine the sugar and butter; beat with an electric mixer on medium speed for 4 to 5 minutes or until fluffy. Add in the egg, beating until well combined and then beat in the vanilla. Adjust your mixer's speed to low and add in 1/3 of the flour mixture and ¼ cup of buttermilk; beat. Continue until all of the flour and buttermilk have been incorporated into the batter. Use a spatula to make sure that no dry ingredients remain on the sides or bottom of the bowl.

- Scoop 6 mounds of batter onto each prepared baking sheet – about 1/3 cup per mound should be about right. Make sure to give the cakes plenty of room in the oven – space them 2 to 3 inches apart. Bake the cakes in the preheated oven for about 15 minutes or until they are springy to touch. Halfway through baking, rotate the pans to ensure even baking. Allow the cakes to cool on the baking sheets for 1 hour before topping with filling and assembling.

- To make the filling, combine the butter and sugar in a mixing bowl and beat with an electric mixer on medium speed until fluffy. Add the vanilla and salt; beat. Then add in the fluff, beating until all of it has been well incorporated. Place the filling in the refrigerator for 30 to 60 minutes to give it a chance to firm up a bit.

- To prepare the cakes, scoop 1/3 cup of the filling onto the center of 6 of the cooled cakes. Place the flat side of an un-topped cake on top, gently pressing just so that the filling reaches the edge of the cake. If using, top with a sprinkle of confectioner's sugar before serving.

# S'more

1927

So special to Americans that they have their own holiday (August 10th), the S'more is a beloved campfire favorite that has made it's way to backyard grills, apartment microwaves, and to the freezers in our favorite ice cream. The Girl Scouts claim credit for inventing the S'more (literally "some more" because that's what everyone wants after finishing the first), the very first recipe for this All-American treat popping up in a 1927 recipe book published by the organization. Whether they invented them or popularized them is unknown, but the companies that sell graham crackers and chocolate bars (oh, and the marshmallows!) are sure glad they did.

This cake captures all of the delicious flavors of the S'more – no campfire necessary, although digging into this cake in front of one is most definitely encouraged.

## S'MORE CAKE
*Serves 10*

### Ingredients
- ★ 4 ounces bittersweet chocolate, finely chopped
- ★ ½ cup heavy cream
- ★ ¼ cup light corn syrup
- ★ 1 cup crushed graham crackers
- ★ 8 graham crackers, broken along dotted lines (24 total)
- ★ 4 tablespoons unsalted butter, melted

* ★ 1 tablespoon sugar
* ★ 1 cup marshmallow cream
* ★ 1 ½ quarts chocolate ice cream, softened
* ★ 2 dozen large marshmallows, halved across

## Directions

- In a medium, microwave-safe bowl combine the chocolate, cream, and corn syrup; melt for 30 seconds then stir and melt for another 30 seconds until completely melted. Allow the mixture to cool for 20 to 30 minutes until it is at room temperature.

- Heat your oven's temperature to 325 degrees F. Prepare a 9" round springform pan by greasing it and lining the sides with parchment paper. In a mixing bowl use your fingers to mix together the graham cracker crumbs, butter, and sugar. Press this mixture into the bottom of the prepared pan and bake in the oven for 10 to 12 minutes or until the crust begins to brown. Allow the crust to cool completely.

- Once the crust is ready, pour the chocolate mixture in, smoothing with a slightly damp spatula; place in the freezer for 30 minutes to firm up. Use a spatula to create a smooth layer of marshmallow cream on top and place in the freezer for another 15 minutes. Then create a layer of ice cream, smoothing the top with a spatula. Use plastic wrap to cover the pan and place in the freezer for 4 to 6 hours.

- Turn on your oven's broiler, moving the top rack so that it sits 6 to 8 inches from the broiler. Set the frozen cake on a baking sheet (remove the plastic wrap). Place the marshmallow halves on top of the ice cream, cut side down. The marshmallows should be very close together. Set the cake under the broiler for no more than 60 seconds so that the marshmallows begin to look lightly toasted. If necessary, turn the cake around halfway 20 to 30 seconds after setting under the broiler. If you are not serving the cake immediately, place back in the freezer.

- Remove the ring from the springform pan and the parchment paper lining the sides. Use the quartered graham crackers to line the sides of the cake, placing them vertically side-by-side; serve immediately.

# Brown Derby Grapefruit

★ ★ ★ ★ ★ ★ ★ ★ ★ ★ ★

1929

Two things attracted customers to the Brown Derby restaurant in Los Angeles when it opened: good food and celebrities. The original Brown Derby opened in 1929 on Wilshire across from the Ambassador hotel. Over time more Brown Derbies opened around the Los Angeles area, strategically placed to coax Hollywood's stars to the watering hole. For example, one Brown Derby, on the corner of Hollywood and Vine, was located by a network radio show broadcast station, which meant that after celebrities did the show for the East Coast they would pop over to Brown Derby and then back to the station for the West Coast show.

The Cobb Salad helped to put the Brown Derby on the foodie map, being acclaimed as one of the best on the West Coast. But more memorable and more original than the Cobb was Brown Derby's Grapefruit Cake, which is still the most popular item in Brown Derby restaurants across the United States. Of course nothing brought more attention to the Brown Derby than the famous 1955 I Love Lucy episode where the gang heads to the restaurant to try to catch a glimpse of the dreamy William Holden.

BROWN DERBY'S GRAPEFRUIT CAKE
*Serves 10*

Ingredients
- ★ 1½ cups cake flour, sifted
- ★ ¾ cup granulated sugar

- ★ 1½ teaspoons baking powder
- ★ ¾ teaspoon salt
- ★ ¼ cup water
- ★ ¼ cup vegetable oil
- ★ 3 large eggs, separated
- ★ 3½ tablespoons freshly squeezed grapefruit juice
- ★ ½ teaspoon grated lemon peel
- ★ ¼ teaspoon cream of tartar

For the frosting

- ★ 6 ounces cream cheese, softened
- ★ 2½ teaspoons freshly squeezed lemon juice
- ★ 1 teaspoon grated lemon peel
- ★ ¾ cup powdered sugar, sifted
- ★ 2 teaspoons crushed grapefruit
- ★ 1 grapefruit, peeled and sectioned

Directions

- Preheat your oven's temperature to 350 degrees F.

- In a large bowl, sift together the flour, sugar, baking powder and salt. Use your fingers to make a well in the middle and add in the water, oil, egg yolks, grapefruit juice, and grated lemon peel. Use an electric mixer to beat until smooth.

- In a separate large bowl, beat the egg whites with the cream of tartar until they hold stiff peaks – just be careful to not over-mix. Transfer the egg yolk mixture into this bowl and fold in with a spatula. Pour the batter into a 9" round springform pan and bake in the preheated oven for 30 minutes or until the top of the cake is springy. Invert the cake onto a cooling rack (leaving the ring around the edges) and cool completely. Once cool, carefully remove the ring to free the cake.

- Make the frosting by placing the cream cheese in a mixing bowl and beating until light and fluffy. Beat in the lemon juice and lemon peel. Then add in the sugar and crushed grapefruit; blend until combined.

- Use a sharp serrated knife to cut the cake to make 2 layers. Spread 1/3 of the frosting on top of the first cake layer and top with pieces of grapefruit. Place the second layer on top and frost the top and sides with remaining frosting, decorating with additional grapefruit sections as desired.

# Depression

1930

During the Great Depression, when money was scarce and supplies, such as food, limited The United States Food Administration distributed pamphlets with the heading "War Economy Food". These handouts encouraged American citizens during the 1930's to reduce their consumption of sugar-laden sweets, asking bakers to instead use items such as molasses, corn, syrup and raisins. Depression Cakes, also known as War Cakes, in addition to using little to no sugar, also reduced or excluded common cake ingredients such as milk, butter, and eggs, considering their expense and availability during this time. Recipes began to circulate, with the help of Betty Crocker, for Depression Cakes advertised to be budget and family-friendly.

## MINNESOTA DEPRESSION CAKE
*Serves 12*

### Ingredients
* ★ 1 cup firmly packed light brown sugar
* ★ 2 cups water
* ★ 1/3 cup vegetable oil
* ★ 2 ½ cups raisins
* ★ 2 ¼ teaspoons ground cinnamon
* ★ ½ teaspoon ground cloves
* ★ 1 teaspoon baking soda
* ★ 1 teaspoon salt

★  2 teaspoons water
★  2 cups flour
★  1 teaspoon baking powder

## Directions

- Set your oven's temperature to 325 degrees F. Grease a 9" square baking pan and set aside. In a large saucepan, combine the sugar, water, oil, raisins, and spices; bring to a boil. Allow the mixture to boil for a few minutes as you stir. Remove the pan from the heat, transfer to a mixing bowl, and cool for 10 minutes.

- In a small bowl, combine the baking soda, salt, and 2 teaspoons of water, stirring until dissolved. Pour this mixture into the cooled raisin mixture, allowing it to foam. Add the flour and baking powder and mix with an electric mixer until well combined. Pour this batter into your prepared baking pan and bake in the preheated oven for about an hour or until a toothpick inserted into the center of the cake comes out clean.

- Allow the cake to cool in its pan for 10 to 20 minutes before slicing and serving.

★ ★ ★ ★ ★ ★ ★ ★ ★ ★

JAPAN ATTACKS PEARL HARBOR AND U.S.
DECLARES WAR DURING WORLD WAR II
1941

COLD WAR BEGINS
1948

★ ★ ★ ★ ★ ★ ★ ★ ★ ★

# Bundt

## 1950

The story goes that in 1950 a group of women from Minneapolis approached a certain H. David Dalquist, an associate of Nordic Ware, asking him to create an affordable pan styled after the traditional European kugelhupf cake pan. Known for its fancy flutes, the kugelhupf pan was made of cast-iron and difficult to find in the United States, and, if found, would cost an arm and a leg to take home. Obliging, Dalquist created an aluminum version of the kugelhupf, but only made a handful, enough for the small group of women who approached him and a few extra for any interested public. Unfortunately, it would take ten years for the public to perk up to the idea of what was being called "The Bundt Pan". When the 1960 edition of the Good Housekeeping Cookbook was published demonstrating the ultimate Bundt Cake, The Tunnel of Fudge, the Bundt Pan began to fly off the shelves and an avalanche of scrumptious recipes using the novel new kitchen tool ensued.

## CHOCOLATE BOURBON BUNDT CAKE
*Serves 14*

### Ingredients

- ★ 1 cup unsweetened cocoa powder + additional for dusting pans
- ★ 1 ½ cups strong brewed coffee
- ★ ½ cup American bourbon
- ★ 1 cup unsalted butter, cut into pieces
- ★ 2 cups granulated sugar

★ 2 cups all-purpose flour
★ 1 ¼ teaspoons baking soda
★ ¼ teaspoon salt
★ 2 large brown eggs
★ 1 ¼ teaspoons vanilla extract
★ Confectioner's sugar, for topping

Directions

- Preheat your oven's temperature to 325 degrees F. Grease a 10" bundt pan and dust with cocoa powder; set aside.

- Combine the coffee, bourbon, and cup of cocoa powder in a 3-quart saucepan. Heat the pan over medium heat and whisk until the butter melts. Take the saucepan off the heat and whisk in the sugar. Once the sugar dissolves pour the mixture into a large bowl and let stand for 5 to 10 minutes.

- Meanwhile, in a mixing bowl combine the flour, baking soda, and salt; whisk. In a separate small bowl whisk together the eggs and vanilla; pour this mixture into the cooled coffee/chocolate mixture and whisk. Then whisk in the flour mixture to create a thin batter. Pour the batter into your prepared bundt pan and bake in the preheated oven for about 45 minutes or until a toothpick inserted into the center of the cake comes out clean.

- Allow the cake to cool in its pan on a wire rack for at least 2 hours before removing it from the pan. Transfer the cooled cake to a serving platter and dust with confectioner's sugar before slicing.

SUPREME COURT MANDATES THAT
SCHOOLS DESEGREGATE
1955

THE CIVIL RIGHTS MOVEMENT BEGINS
1960

# Tunnel Of Fudge

## 1960

The cake that put the Bundt pan on the map, The Tunnel of Fudge cake, created by Ella Helfrich of Texas, came in second place in the 1960 Pillsbury Bake-Off. But to the good folks at Nordic Ware, the creation of this cake will always be a grand-prize winner in their eyes. A product that was so off the radar that people wouldn't accept it as a gift, after the publication of the Tunnel of Fudge recipe Bundt pans flew off the shelves and they still do to this day.

## THE TUNNEL OF FUDGE CAKE
*Serves 12*

### Ingredients

- ★ ½ cup boiling water
- ★ 2 ounces bittersweet chocolate, chopped
- ★ 2 ¼ cups all-purpose flour
- ★ 2 cups walnuts, finely chopped
- ★ 2 cups confectioner's sugar
- ★ ¾ cup Dutch cocoa powder + additional for pans
- ★ ¾ teaspoon salt
- ★ 20 tablespoons unsalted butter, softened
- ★ 1 cup granulated sugar
- ★ ¾ cup light brown sugar, packed
- ★ 1 tablespoon pure vanilla extract
- ★ 5 large eggs, at room temperature

For the glaze

- ★ 4 ounces bittersweet chocolate, melted
- ★ ½ cup heavy cream, hot
- ★ 2 tablespoons light corn syrup
- ★ ¼ teaspoon vanilla extract

Directions

- Preheat your oven's temperature to 350 degrees F. Grease a nonstick 3-quart Bundt pan with melted butter and dust with cocoa powder; set aside.

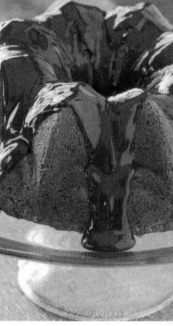

- In a small bowl combine the boiling water and chocolate and whisk until smooth – cool for 3 to 5 minutes. In a medium bowl combine the flour, nuts, confectioner's sugar, cocoa powder, and salt; whisk to combine.

- In a mixing bowl cream together the butter, sugars, and vanilla with an electric mixer on medium speed. Once the mixture appears fluffy beat in the eggs one at a time. Then beat in the chocolate mixture until incorporated. Adjust the mixer's speed to low and beat in the flour mixture. Pour the mixture into the prepared pan and smooth the top with a spatula. Tap the bottom of the pan on the counter a few times to ensure that no air pockets are in the batter. Bake the cake in the preheated oven for 45 minutes or until the edges of the cake begin to pull away from the sides of the pan. You want the cake to be slightly under-baked to achieve the gooey, fudge center this cake is famous for.

- As the cake bakes create the glaze by combining all of the ingredients in a medium bowl with a whisk. When finished, the glaze should look thick and smooth.

- Let the cake cool in its pan for 10 minutes before removing from the pan. Allow the cake to cool on a wire rack for 2 to 3 hours before drizzling with the glaze. Wait 20 to 30 minutes for the glaze to set before slicing and serving.

★ ★ ★ ★ ★ ★ ★ ★ ★ ★

THE USE OF DDT AS A PESTICIDE IS
BANNED IN THE UNITED STATES
1972

★ ★ ★ ★ ★ ★ ★ ★ ★ ★

# Jell-O Poke

1976

It's no surprise that this cake was invented by the Jell-O Company as a clever marketing ploy. In a 1976 advertising pamphlet, Jell-O piqued the interest of consumers with its recipe for its Poke Cake, which required bakers to poke holes in the top of a baked cake and then pour hot, liquid gelatin mixture all over their beautiful cake. A novel (and to many weird) idea turned into a phenomenon as bakers realized the limitless possibilities behind this method of cake making. School colors, holiday themes, the Jell-O Poke cake offered a creative outlet for bakers across America.

## PATRIOTIC POKE CAKE
*Serves 16*

### Ingredients

★ 2/3 cup whole milk, at room temperature
★ 4 large egg whites, at room temperature
★ 1 ½ teaspoons pure vanilla extract
★ 1½ cups cake flour
★ 1 cup + 2 tablespoons granulated sugar
★ 2½ teaspoons baking powder
★ ½ teaspoon salt
★ 8 tablespoons unsalted butter, softened and cooled

For the Jell-O
- ★ 1 cup fresh strawberries, husked
- ★ ¼ cup water
- ★ 2/3 cup granulated sugar
- ★ 2¼ teaspoons strawberry gelatin
- ★ ¾ cup fresh blueberries
- ★ ½ cup water
- ★ 4 ½ teaspoons granulated sugar
- ★ 4 ½ teaspoons blue gelatin

For the frosting and filling
- ★ 2 ½ cups heavy whipping cream
- ★ 1/3 cup confectioner's sugar

Directions
- Preheat your oven to 350 degrees F. Prepare two 8" round cake pans by greasing and flouring; set aside.

- In a small bowl combine the milk, egg whites, and vanilla. In a large mixing bowl beat on low speed the flour, sugar, baking powder, and salt (or simply whisk). Then add the butter and cream for 1 minute. Pour in half of the milk mixture and beat on medium speed until the batter looks smooth. Continue beating and add in the remaining milk; beat for 30 seconds or until the batter looks fluffy. Divide the mixture evenly between the 2 prepared pans and bake in the preheated oven for about 25 minutes or until a toothpick inserted into the center of the cakes comes out clean. Allow the cakes to cool completely in their pans on top of wire racks.

- To prepare the strawberry Jell-o, place the strawberries, water, and sugar in a small saucepan and bring to a boil. Reduce the heat and allow the mixture to simmer for a few minutes. When finished the strawberries should be tender. Strain the mixture into a small bowl; discard pulp. Then stir in the gelatin until dissolved and cool the mixture to room temperature.

- Follow this same procedure to prepare the blue gelatin.

- Once the cakes have cooled, use a wooden skewer to poke holes in the tops of the cakes, not poking any within 1" of the edges. Pour the strawberry gelatin over the top of one cake and the blue gelatin over the top of the other. Place the cakes covered with plastic wrap in the refrigerator overnight.

- Prepare the frosting and filling by beating the cream in a large bowl. Once thickened, beat in the confectioner's sugar until the mixture holds soft peaks.

- Use a small knife to remove the cakes from the pans. Place the strawberry cake on the bottom layer and top with 1 cup of the whipped filling. Place the blue Jell-O cake on top and frost the top and sides with the remaining whipped filling/frosting. Allow the cake to stand in the refrigerator for 1 to 2 hours before slicing and serving.

THE FIRST PERSONAL COMPUTER
IS CREATED
1978

NASA LANDS A SPACECRAFT
ON MARS
1997

# Coca-Cola

1997

A delicious accident was the invention of the Coca-Cola cake. In 1997, The Cracker Barrel team was discussing ways to incorporate more of the classic soda into their menu. They, like many chain restaurants, hired outside companies to develop new Coca-Cola recipes. With the idea of a dessert in mind, several of these companies began to toy with variations of the Coca-Cola Cake. One company, misreading the sample recipe, more than doubled the amount of cocoa required to make the cake. A happy mistake thankfully as the Cracker Barrel executives and their posse loved it and added it to their menu as a seasonal special.

But limited availability proved too much to handle by the hardcore Coca-Cola Cake fans that wrote letters to Cracker Barrel requesting that the cake be put on the menu full time. In 2009 it finally happened and the cake remained on the menu for the entire year. An immediate best seller, the cake now has a permanent home in the 622 Cracker Barrel restaurants now open in the United States.

## COPY CAT CHOCOLATE COCA-COLA CAKE
*Serves 10*

### Ingredients
- ★ 1 cup Coca-Cola
- ★ ½ cup vegetable oil
- ★ ½ cup unsalted butter

★  3 tablespoons cocoa powder
★  2 cups granulated sugar
★  2 ¼ cups flour
★  ¼ teaspoon salt
★  2 large eggs
★  ½ cup buttermilk
★  1 teaspoon baking soda
★  1 teaspoon vanilla extract

For the frosting
★  8 tablespoons unsalted butter
★  3 tablespoons cocoa powder
★  6 tablespoons milk
★  1 ¼ teaspoons pure vanilla extract
★  ½ cup pecans, chopped (optional)
★  4¾ cups confectioner's sugar

Directions

- Preheat your oven to 350 degrees F.  Prepare a 9x13" cake pan by greasing the bottom and sides and then dusting with flour – set aside.

- In a large saucepan combine the Coca-Cola, oil, butter, and cocoa powder and heat to a boil.  Then add in the sugar, flour, and salt mixing well and then bringing it to a boil.  Pour the boiling mixture into a mixing bowl and beat with an electric mixer to cool slightly. Then beat in the eggs, buttermilk, baking soda, and vanilla extract.  Pour the batter into the prepared cake pan and bake in the preheated oven for about 25 minutes or until a toothpick inserted into the center comes out clean.  Allow the cake to cool in its pan while you make the frosting.

- Combine the butter, cocoa powder, and milk in a medium saucepan over medium heat.   Once the butter melts transfer the mixture to a mixing bowl. Use an electric mixer to beat in the remaining frosting ingredients.  When finished, the frosting should look glossy and smooth.

- Spread the frosting on top of the cooled cake before serving and slicing.

# One American Family's Photo History Of Cakes

★ ★ ★ ★ ★ ★ ★ ★ ★ ★ ★

## (With Clever Tips And Tricks!)

Cakes have always been a big deal in my family. Looking back I can almost say with complete confidence that for the first twenty years of my life a cake was baked and consumed in my home at least once a week. There was always a reason for cake (and thank goodness for that!) Here are some of the most memorable cakes from my family's past to peruse, enjoy, and hopefully inspire your next Baking Betty adventure!

*My grandparents in their kitchen about to enjoy a birthday cake in 1980*

My family has a tradition of adding up the two numbers in the birthday's person age (for example, 58 is 5+8) in order to conserve candles, space, and prevent the table catching on fire. My parents and grandparents have been observing this tradition for as long as I can remember; my siblings and I reluctant to accept that we are getting older still get all (thirty plus) candles on our birthday cakes.

*My parents' cake on their wedding day, August 8, 1980*

My mom is incredible. Both this wedding cake and her dress she handmade for their special day. The tradition continues as she has made my and my two sisters' beautiful wedding cakes, which kept her very busy considering we got married in the summers of 2009, 2010, and 2011. My brothers and dad loved the fact that wedding cake requires lots of practice runs, keeping their bellies filled with cake for nearly three years (not that that is unusual for our family though!)

*My sister Karen's homemade wedding cake, May 23, 2009*

*My homemade wedding cake, July 2, 2010*

*My sister Shelley's homemade wedding cake for her reception in the mountains, May 5, 2011*

Like most American families the highlight of our parties is the cake. It is very rare that a cake is purchased for a birthday. Instead, requests are put in to my mom (sometimes months in advance) and she graciously obliges, turning out some of the most beautiful and personalized cakes like there's nothing to it. And when we're finished eating, there really is nothing...

*My 7ᵗʰ birthday cake made from a popular doll cake mold my mom found at the local hobby store and decorated with a dress of my favorite color, May 26, 1995*

*Me on my 13th birthday with a hand-drawn flamingo cake, May 26, 2001*

*My sister Shelley with a hand-decorated cake on her 21st birthday, March 2, 2003. The candles were placed on the cake after the picture was taken.*

*My brother Ryan's 6th birthday cake made from a store-bought dog cake pan and painstakingly hand-decorated with various tips on a decorator's bag, July 18, 2003*

*My mom with her birthday cake decorated in fall colors, decorator's bag roses, and a simple ribbon around the edge, September 2005*

*Not your typical birthday cake, for my 16th birthday I requested a sheet of Rice Krispie Treats frosted like a cake with a store-bought edible Barbie decal, May 26, 2005*

*Ryan's 8th birthday cake, a chocolate marble sheet cake with chocolate frosting and his favorite cartoon characters, July 18, 2005*

*My dad with his repurposed birthday cake – that year my mom made tons of sheet cakes for my brother's high school, not wanting to waste what was left, she re-decorated it with birthday candles. Since the cake was so delicious no one minded that it had been cut in half, November 2008*

*Ryan with an ice cream cake for his fourteenth birthday. To make the ice cream cake my mom bakes a sheet cake, uses a serrate knife to carefully cut it in half to make two layers, spreads softened ice cream like frosting in the middle, frosts with regular frosting on the top and sides, and then places in the freezer for several hours before serving, July18, 2011*

*My sister Karen with her birthday cake for her 27<sup>th</sup> birthday, November 7, 2011*

*My sister, Shelley's, birthday and her brother-in-law, Rory's, birthday are just a few days apart. In 2012 the families decided to throw a joint birthday party with all of their friends, my mom responsible for the cakes. Rory is a huge Green Bay Packer's fan so with the help of the local bakery she printed out an edible Packer logo. My sister, who plays tennis, had a similar edible decal printed out for her cake. The scoreboards displayed by each cake show their birthdays and the game clock shows their age, March 2012*

*Me with a chocolate cookies and cream ice cream cake for my 25ᵗʰ birthday, May 26, 2012*

*My sister Karen with her birthday cake for her 28ᵗʰ birthday, November 2012*

*My brother Alex with his birthday cake for his 20th birthday, April 28, 2013*

*Working on recipes for my sister's brother-in-law's wedding, my mom baked herself this chiffon cake decorated with fresh raspberries and homegrown geraniums for her birthday, September 17, 2013*

The Easter Bunny Cake is a tradition in my family, one made every year for dessert after our Easter lunch. The cake is cleverly made with two round cakes. One round cake stays in tact for the bunny's face; the other cake is turned into a bow tie and two ears. Here are a few of our favorite "Bunny Cakes" over the years.

*My sister Karen with our family's Easter cake in 2001*

*Our flirtatious Easter Bunny in 2003*

*Our freckled bunny decorated with Skittles, sprinkles, Red Hots, and jellybeans in 2005*

*Twizzler pull-apart candies helped to decorate the Bunny Cake in 2006*

Most Americans indulge in sweets on Valentine's Day – my family's dessert of choice is, of course, cake. The cake pictured below is not made with a heart-shaped mold. Instead, my mom used a square cake and a round cake. The square cake is turned on a diagonal and the circle cake is cut in half and placed on the top two edges of the square. Color-coordinated heart candies and sprinkles help to make the cake look even more impressive.

*Ryan and my mom with the Valentine's Day cake in 2006*

Beyond weddings, birthdays, and holidays, cakes are enjoyed in my family for a variety of reasons. Admittedly, those reasons have been stretched and exaggerated in the past to coax my mom into trying a new recipe on a regular basis. Over the years my mom's cakes have become famous in our town, with requests coming in for parties and celebrations of all sorts. Once word got out, people would call my mom before calling a bakery – and never went back.

*This cake was made for my family's dog's birthday. The cake looks like Fremont with the spot in the center of his head and spots that really did look like the word "Boo", May 25, 1995*

*A large, double-chocolate sheet cake made for my sister Karen's high school graduation party,*
*May 2003*

*My brother Alex won his school Spelling Bee in the fifth grade.  This cake was waiting for him*
*when he got home from school, December 2004*

*Before my high school soccer team's first State Championship game, my mom had the team over for dinner and served this half-chocolate-half-vanilla cake for dessert, October 2005*

*My high school class had a party at the local pool to celebrate our graduation. My mom was in charge in making enough cakes for close to two hundred people. This is one of several of the cakes she carefully boxed and brought to the pool, May 2006*

*My sister Karen and her future husband Dominic studied at a university in Guadalajara, Mexico in 2006. For their welcome home party, my mom went to the local bakery to have them custom print a picture onto edible rice paper. She then applied the photo to her cake, along with roses made with a decorator tip and hardened in the freezer, August 2006*

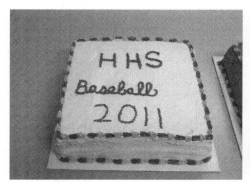

*Rather than purchase cakes from the bakery, which can be expensive, my brother's high school baseball team commissioned my mom to bake the cakes for the team's Awards Banquet. One vanilla and one chocolate, there wasn't a single slice left at the end of the night, May 2011*

*My brother Alex with the cake my mom made for his high school graduation party decorated in his high school's colors and with memorabilia from the sports he played, baseball, basketball, and soccer, May 2011*

# Discover More Great Books at

Little Pearl Publishing
(and don't forget to tell a friend!)

Printed in Great Britain
by Amazon